The Rope Trick

Close Your Eyes and Open Your Mind To Better Know Your Relationships

Will Cupchik Ph.D.

ISBN: 978-1-896342-14-6

Published by Tagami Communications, 2528 Bayview Avenue, P.O. Box 35532, Toronto, Ontario, Canada M2L 2Y4.

Manufactured in the United States.

Printed on acid-free paper.

BookLocker.com, Inc. 2015

2015 September 2015 2nd Printing.

Cupchik,Will, 1940-
title [electronic resource] :
/ Will Cupchik.

Includes bibliographical references.
  1. Relationships
  2. Relationships - assessment and treatment
  3. Mental imagery exercise
  4. The Rope Trick mental imagery exercise
  5. Clinical Imaginative Imagery – doctoral dissertation, University of Toronto

Cover photo by Worasak Charung; Licensed from Dreamstime.com

DISCLAIMERS

This book presents information pertaining to the *Cupchik Rope Trick*, a powerful mental imagery exercise that has been demonstrated to be one of the easiest and fastest ways to gain insight into the current status and dynamics of a personal or work-related relationship. I created this exercise in the 1970s to help a therapy client who was having a great deal of difficulty understanding and describing her marital relationship. Genuinely surprised by its evident potency, I rigorously examined *how* and *why* the Rope Trick worked so well by devoting my doctoral thesis to this subject within the Counselling Psychology section of the *Department of Graduate Studies* at the University of Toronto.

Please note that the full copyrighted name of this exercise is the *Cupchik Rope Trick mental imagery exercise©*, although throughout most of this book it will simply be referred to as the *Rope Trick mental imagery exercise©*, the *Rope Trick exercise©*, or simply as the *Rope Trick©*. I am very careful to give credit to the creators of any of the various psychotherapeutic tools that I employ [the *Karpman* Drama Triangle, the *Gouldings'* Redecision Therapy, and so on…] and would certainly appreciate it if professionals who choose to use the *Rope Trick* with their clients would acknowledge *its* originator.

The author and publisher are providing this book and its contents on an "as is" basis and make no warranties of any kind with respect to this book or its contents. The author and publisher disclaim all such representations and warranties, including for example warranties of merchantability and healthcare for a particular purpose or individual. In addition, the author and publisher do not represent or warrant that the information accessible via this book is accurate, complete or current.

The statements made about products and services have not been evaluated by the U.S. Food and Drug Administration. They are not intended to diagnose, treat, cure, or prevent any condition or disease.

iii

Please consult with your own physician, healthcare specialist and/or psychotherapist regarding the suggestions and recommendations made in this book.

Neither the author or publisher, nor any other representatives will be liable for damages arising out of, or in connection with, the use of this book. This is a comprehensive limitation of liability that applies to all damages of any kind, including [without limitation] compensatory; direct, indirect or consequential damages; loss of data, income or profit; loss of or damage to property, relationships or claims of third parties.

You understand that this book is not intended as a substitute for a thorough consultation with a suitably trained and experienced psychotherapist. Before you begin any healthcare-oriented exercise or program, or change your life or lifestyle in any way, you should consult your physician or other licensed healthcare practitioner to ensure that you are in good health and that the examples, exercises and recommendations and/or suggestions contained in this book will not harm you.

It is important to realize that in carrying out the Rope Trick mental imagery exercise, what you may find might not be at all what you had expected, and **if you are not ready to accept the mental imagery experience as possibly having some however uncomfortable significance, you would be well advised to NOT carry out the exercise**.

In all instances you should only consider using the Rope Trick mental imagery exercise if you are currently in treatment with a suitably experienced and qualified psychotherapist, one who familiar with the symbolic interpretation of dreams.

Neither the author/creator of the Rope Trick© exercise and Bridge Trick© exercise, nor the publisher of this book, shall bear any responsibility for the productions of the exercises produced by any individual, their specific interpretations or any consequences that might follow.

This book provides content related to physical and/or mental health issues. As such, use of this book implies your acceptance of this disclaimer.

Please note: **At the time of the publication of this second printing of this book, a spoken rendition of the Rope Trick mental imagery exercise had been posted on YouTube at https://www.youtube. com/watch?v=bdXyfAbY4Ag** *read aloud by the author*. **This rendition has been provided for the convenience of individuals who have read this book, and who are aware of the information and precautions provided herein, so that they may just sit back, close their eyes and follow the spoken instructions of the Rope Trick exercise.**

The responsibility for making use of the contents of this book and/or of the YouTube video is the informed user's alone, and only the user shall bear the responsibility for the imagery sequence produced by him or her, its interpretation and any consequences that might follow from its use.

DEDICATION

This book is dedicated to the many hundreds of persons who have experienced firsthand, and in many cases have chosen to share with me their own Rope Trick mental imagery experiences over the past many years, and to you, the reader, because by picking up this book you have likely expressed an interest in learning more about relationships in general and perhaps your own in particular. I'm sure you will find the Rope Trick mental imagery exercise to be fascinating, instructive or at the very least, interesting!

This book is also dedicated to the person for whom I created it during a group therapy session, and whose extraordinarily valuable and insightful experience prompted me to explore this mental imagery exercise's potential further by devoting [as it turned out] nearly five years to a vigorous investigation of its power and value as a major part of my doctoral dissertation.

Barry Simon, M.D., an outstanding psychiatrist and psychoanalyst, and as importantly, a compassionate professional and a mensch, read an earlier draft of this book, has used the Rope Trick and generously shared some valuable suggestions regarding the book, for which I am very grateful.

I am thankful also to **Dr. Mark Minden**, a remarkable physician whose ready and attentive accessibility and considerable expertise have been of so much assistance these past few years. Also, Mark is another mensch whose thoughtful compassion is much appreciated.

My long-time friend, **Judith Rockert**, read an earlier draft of this book and offered salient feedback that I have attempted to incorporate in this version. Jude was right on about the title of this book, as well. I am grateful, also, for her many efforts on my behalf generally, and for her dear, dear friendship these past more than thirty years.

I also want to acknowledge the efforts of my friend **Rena Godfrey** in helping to promote the public's awareness of this book.

Two other very close friends of about twenty-five years, psychologist and engineer **Dr. Jack Lin**, the co-founder of National Technical Systems headquartered in L.A., and **David Martin**, an exceptional and psychologically informed architect from Monterey, California, have been steady sources of support for me generally, and my professional endeavours in particular. Their friendships have meant a great deal to me over the years – likely more than they realize. Whenever we 'three amigos' have come together to help facilitate our own –and each others'- growth, the results have most often been very memorable – and highly gratifying.

I would be most remiss if I did not express my sincere but belated thanks to psychologists **Drs. Ron Langevin, Dvora Levinson** and **Ruth Bray** for their great assistance during the course of my doctoral investigations. Dr. Langevin deserves considerable additional thanks for the most generous assistance he provided to me via the main University of Toronto computer and for providing me with very insightful mock orals whereby his feedback about my being 'on' or 'off' in my responses were so very obvious to him and helped me to decide how to best approach the task of the final Senate oral. Dr. Levinson has been a consistent colleague and steadfast friend for over four decades, and I am very appreciative of both kinds of relationships that we have shared.

My awesome step-son, **Matthew**, himself an excellent writer and editor, lent his incisive expertise to helping me finally decide on an appropriate title and subtitle for this book. I am also very thankful to be blessed with my remarkable daughter-in-law **Sorelle**, and my fabulous grandchildren, **Shia**, **Essie**, **Levi**, **Nechama** and **Yosef**, who give me such pleasure and joy by simply being themselves.

As has been true of my earlier books, I am again grateful to my extraordinary wife, **Barbara**, a published writer in her own right, for her unfailing support during the creation of this book, for her thorough reading of some earlier drafts and for our frequent consultations about this and my other writing professional projects. Barb has also provided me with an exceptional extended family, for which I will always be very grateful.

TABLE OF CONTENTS

LIST OF CASES

Case # 1: Lynda, the first ever user of the rope trick mental imagery exercise.

Case # 2: Mary and the noose.

Case # 3: David and the skipping rope.

Case # 4: Bill: a most delicate rope trick example: one end of the rope was tied around his Ph.D. supervisor's 'private parts'

Case # 5: Wayne, a passive, unassertive partner.

Case # 6: Claire, the single, 50 year old client who never had more than three dates with the same man… and the missing rope.

Case # 7: Hank and Nadine, a young married couple who came to counseling too late.

Case # 8: Sam & Veronica: 28 years of a deteriorating marriage was too much.

Case # 9: Tom and the possible symbolic meaning of the seemingly unreasonable demand of his now-adult son [who at the time was married with children of his own].

Case # 10: Harriet, whose 'bridge trick" exercise was right on!

Case # 11: Victor, an honest man whose seemingly nonsensical act of shoplifting clearly demonstrated the symbolic meaning of *what* he stole, *when* and *why*.

AUTHOR'S PERSONAL NOTE

When I was still in high school and wondering what profession I would like to pursue, I whittled down my most desirable options to two seemingly very different paths - either becoming an electrical engineer or a psychologist. At the age of sixteen I decided that I would first study one of these professions at the university level, practice it for a while, then perhaps return to university to undertake studies for the *other* profession, practice *it* for a time, and then make up my mind as to which of the two career options interested me most. I would not recommend that most people follow such a circuitous path, but in my case it turned out to be a good idea, since engineering gave me a solid grounding in a hard science and in my first and only job as a graduate engineer I designed navigational guidance systems for the then-next generation of military aircraft for the United States and other NATO countries. These studies and work helped to train my mind to create and follow experimental designs, and I was several years older and somewhat more mature when I began to study psychology in earnest.

I earned a Bachelor of Engineering degree in electrical engineering [electronics option] from McGill University in 1961. During the five-year engineering degree program my courses exposed me to some of the then latest scientific information in atomic physics. After graduation, I was fortunate to obtain what was undoubtedly one of the very best engineering jobs available anywhere in the country at that time; I was hired as a Navigation Systems Design engineer at Computing Devices of Canada [later bought by the Bendix Corporation of the United States, which itself was later acquired by Raytheon and other corporate entities] and worked developing hardware that allowed ship-based, anti-submarine-seeking helicopters to carry out their search manoeuvres, all the while maintaining an electronic awareness of their positions (or relationships) relative to each other as well as their 'mother' ships. These systems were ultimately purchased by the United States Navy as well as other NATO countries.

At the time of publication of this book I have been a Registered Psychologist and a member of the American Psychological Association, Canadian Psychological Association and Ontario Psychological Association for over 35 years and am currently an honorary life member of all three professional organizations.

In recent years, as I have reflected upon my more than 54 years of professional employment, I became aware of the fact that in both engineering and psychology, my professional efforts have been aimed at dealing with the relationships of either one object [for example, a helicopter] to another object [for instance, an aircraft carrier], or the relationship of one person to another person, which is what much of counseling psychology in general, and the Rope Trick mental imagery exercise in particular, are about.

Over the past more than 40 years I have offered the Rope Trick to many hundreds of persons within in my own psychotherapy practice, and also presented it at international conferences and numerous workshops. As a result, this book is based upon a vast richness of experience, and especially as I have used the Rope Trick with individuals and couples from more than 20 countries and cultures.

I am also the author of three non-fiction books in my *forensic* specialty which deals with the atypical theft behavior of usually honest persons [individuals who are too frequently misdiagnosed as suffering from kleptomania]. My books, ***Why Honest People Shoplift Or Commit Other Acts Of Theft*** [1997; Revised Ed., 2002] and ***Why Usually Honest People Steal*** [2013] are currently available from online bookstores. My latest book in this field, tentatively titled, ***The Clinician's Manual: The Assessment And Treatment Of Usually Honest People Who Shoplift Or Commit Other Bizarre Thefts***, as well as my soon to be reissued novel, tentatively titled **Murdering Medicare: The Avro Arrow Manipulation.**

PREFACE

THIS BOOK IS INTENDED FOR THE USE OF BOTH LAYPERSONS AND PSYCHOTHERAPISTS

A note for laypersons:

Laypersons, i.e., for our purposes any individuals who are *not* practicing or former mental health professionals, may choose to use and interpret the Rope Trick mental imagery exercise on their own [taking into account the information provided in this book], keeping in mind the disclaimers mentioned previously. It is also important to understand that, just as is true of night dreams, the Rope Trick imagery sequences [or 'responses' as they will also be referred to in this book] can have *various* interpretations, none of which should be taken as 'gospel' or presumed to be definitive. Rather, by carrying out the Rope Trick exercise in the manner that is outlined in detail in this book, and with practice, it may well be possible, within a very few minutes or less, to acquire insights into aspects of a relationship that may not have been entirely clear to the user beforehand.

A Warning or Caveat: it is *always* advisable to review one's Rope Trick exercise response with an experienced psychotherapist who is knowledgeable in the interpretations of dreams and the possible meanings of symbols. Neither the author nor publisher accepts any responsibility for any imagery sequences or the consequences of same that may be experienced and/or interpreted by any user or his or her psychotherapist. If a reader is unsure whether he or she would be ready or able to deal with the resulting imagery and/or interpretations of the Rope Trick exercise, then that person would be well advised to <u>not</u> carry out the exercise without the assistance of a qualified psychotherapist.

In order to make for easier reading, the main parts of this book are written with laypersons in mind. For those who wish to learn even more about mental imagery, the appendices at the back of this book are intended to provide some of this material.

A note for psychotherapists:

The Rope Trick© was thoroughly investigated from within a rigorous experimental design for my doctoral dissertation within the Department of Graduate Studies at the University of Toronto [Ph.D. in granted in 1979]. It was shown to be both clinically <u>valid</u> [i.e., it reveals the current status and dynamics of an interpersonal relationship] and is also <u>reliable</u> in a clinical sense, [i.e., it will likely provide a psychodynamically similar experience, time and again, over a short period and while the qualities of the relationship remains the same]. It should go without saying that, just as is true for any clinical intervention or exercise, the results of its use are neither necessarily predictable, accurate nor valid for *every* user on *every* occasion, and the involvement of a suitably trained clinician is always advisable.

By all means, consider the Rope Trick as a potentially powerful tool to employ with clients who are attempting to deal with their relationships. Even more than forty years on <u>I still usually choose to read aloud to clients the optimal, written version of the Rope Trick experience to clients</u>. This reading assures that each person gets virtually exactly the same mental imagery exercise in nearly the very same way as did the original 40 subjects of my dissertation, and that allows the therapist to pay the most attention to the client's mental imagery production, or 'response', having been assured that the Rope Trick exercise was delivered in the optimal fashion. I have included a verbatim rendition of the Rope Trick to use with clients in Chapter 1.

There is also another important reason why it can be best to read the written version of the Rope Trick to clients. The read-out-loud-from-the-written-version of the Rope Trick showed itself to be especially important in the case of the only person among the 40 who took part in the original experimental design *who did not include a rope in her response* and swore that no mention of a rope was ever provided when the exercise was originally read out to her. Thankfully, not only had the exercise been read in full from the written script but the delivery had also been recorded, and therefore the client could hear for herself that there had indeed been mention of a rope – in fact, five different times, during the presentation of the exercise. This fascinating case is discussed in more detail later on in this book.

The fact that I have so much familiarity with the Rope Trick and so much information about how to interpret it does not appear to have markedly influenced my own response whenever I carry out the exercise. After writing the previous sentence, as an example, I actually did the Rope Trick exercise in regard to a relationship that I happen to be currently intrigued by; my imagery response came very quickly, within about 10 seconds. Probably because I am so familiar with the exercise and how to interpret it, the likely meaning of my response became clear very quickly. At the same time I do not believe that my familiarity with the exercise distorted my response in any substantial way, and the imagery that occurred to me was both instructive and insightful. Many others have similarly reported that having more information about, and practise with, the Rope Trick exercise did not likely lead to manipulating the responses they experienced.

I personally use the Rope Trick mental imagery exercise whenever I want to gain some additional insight into what may be going on in a particular relationship. Do keep in mind that it is a *here-and-now* exercise; at a later time the response I may have when carrying out the exercise is likely to be correspondingly different, reflecting the changes in the relationship that have gone on during the interval.

Please Note: All the case examples presented in this book have been effectively camouflaged as to the identity, names, gender [sometimes] and other idiosyncratic particulars of the persons whose cases are mentioned.

INTRODUCTION: WHAT IS MENTAL IMAGERY?

In layperson's terms, virtually all of us are able to *imagine*, or see with our minds' eye, walking along a favorite beach, playing with a child or grandchild, or looking at a loved one's face. These are *visual* mental images.

Using our minds' ears we may be able to imagine hearing our favorite music, a child's laughter or a best friend saying "hello" when we meet.

These visual and auditory "quasi-sensory experiences" are all example of mental images.

Also, many of us are able to imagine touching a hot stove, feeling the sandpapery-like stubble of a father's or grandfather's cheek, the luxuriousness of incredibly soft fur, or almost any other sensory experience *in the absence of the actual external stimulus*.

These are all examples of mental imagery.

A more formal definition of mental imagery:
For the more academically inclined, mental imagery may be defined as *"those quasi-sensory experiences of which we are self-consciously aware which exist for us in the absence of those stimulus conditions that are known to produce their genuine sensory or perceptual counterparts and which may be expected to have different consequences from their sensory counterparts."* **[Richardson, A., Mental Imagery, New York: Springer Publishing Company, 1969, p.2]**

As mentioned previously, over 40 years ago, while I was co-leading a therapy group for a psychiatrist in private practice, a woman in her early 40s [let us call her 'Lynda'] was becoming increasingly frustrated as she found herself having great difficulty understanding, let alone describing, her at the time, troubling marital relationship. On the spur of the moment I created for her what I assumed was just another minor mental imagery exercise [something I regularly fashioned for clients] that I thought might help Lynda to probe further into her relationship with her husband. Because we were in a *group* therapy session, I invited the other members of the group to also close their eyes, relax and follow my verbal instructions. I was quite surprised, however, when, less than 15 seconds after I had completed the instructions for the exercise, Lynda exclaimed, *"That's it! That's exactly what our relationship is like!"* When she then fully described her imagery experience it seemed obvious that she had indeed had a very illuminating imagery sequence, one that seemed to encapsulate many important aspects of her distressing marital relationship. [Lynda's Rope Trick experience will be discussed in more detail later.]

Interestingly, not only did Lynda have a valuable imagery experience but so did most of the other members of that therapy group. In turn, as several of them described to the rest of us what imagery sequences they had experienced and what they meant to them, it was clear that most had gained useful insights into their respective relationships.

As I also indicated previously, the Rope Trick was so informative about relationships that I decided to devote my doctoral thesis* to vigorously exploring this original mental imagery exercise, why it worked and its validity [that is to say, whether it accurately offered information about the relationship under consideration] and its reliability [i.e., could it be relied upon to provide a similar experience when offered to individuals for a second time a short time later?].

As a former graduate electrical engineer I was already well informed as to how experimental studies are carried out in the so-called 'hard sciences'. With the help of other scientifically oriented psychologist-advisors I developed and carried out a meticulous experimental design that allowed me to study the Rope Trick at a level of scientific investigation that was quite unusual at the time [and

2

perhaps still is] for a mental imagery exercise. The study clearly indicated that the Rope Trick exercise actually can do what it purported to do; that is, it can provide important insights into the current status and dynamics of a relationship at the moment when it is used.

In this book I offer you the full rendition of the Rope Trick exercise [which takes all of about 10 minutes to carry out] and I also provide many clues to help you decode your own imagery response to the exercise. By doing the Rope Trick and then interpreting the results you may find that you would gain important insights into one of your major relationships, and because the exercise can have a therapeutic effect as well, you may also find that your relationship might actually change.

* To explore the Rope Trick exercise thoroughly, many thousands of hours over nearly five years were spent rigorously examining the exercise from within an experimental design. For purposes of my doctoral thesis I offered the Rope Trick or its equivalent to 40 individuals; in each case their experiences were both audio recorded and written down by each of them longhand. A separate tool that I developed and termed the Relationship Questionnaire, was also offered to these same subjects. As well, three psychologists from differing clinical orientations were provided with the written responses of the subjects to the Rope Trick exercise and each was asked to rate the relationships [as were the clients themselves] on the 24 multiple-choice item Relationship Questionnaire that was shown to assess the adequacy of four independent factors of interpersonal relationships: Emotional depth, Balance of control, Mutual dependency and a [Lack of] malice.

The reader will be offered the full Rope Trick mental imagery exercise on the pages that follow. My suggestion is that you consider carrying out the exercise in regard to a relationship of importance to you and preferably one that you would like to better understand at a deeper level at the present time. Do keep in mind that you would be well advised to preferably carry out the Rope Trick only if you are currently in treatment with an experienced psychotherapist who is practised in interpreting the symbolism inherent in night dreams or their equivalent, and only if you are prepared to deal with unexpected and/or potentially upsetting thoughts, emotions and/or insights.

.

Chapter 1

THE FULL AND FORMAL RENDERING OF THE ROPE TRICK EXERCISE

When using this mental imagery exercise, do keep in mind that:

- The actual experience that you have may be quite powerful;

- There are sometimes varying interpretations to be made of a Rope Trick experience and some of them may not be equally as valid as some others;

- It is always wise to consult with an experienced psychotherapist who is very familiar with you and the symbolism of dreams when attempting to interpret the meaning of the experience, and,

- Before making any major or decisive changes in your relationship with the other person as a result of, or in response to, carrying out the Rope Trick exercise, the old carpenter's rule is sound advice; *"Nine times measure and the tenth time cut."* In other words, think long and hard and possibly discuss any major changes being considered [e.g., moving in with - or separating from - that individual] with an independent third party, preferably a suitable psychotherapist.

What follows is a near-identical presentation of the Rope Trick mental imagery exercise that I have given to many hundreds of clients and workshop attendees over the past more than four decades.

5

[Instructions and other notes regarding the delivery of the Rope Trick mental imagery exercise have been placed in brackets, just as has this sentence.]

You, the reader, may best carry out the Rope Trick mental imagery exercise by: [1] recording the following script yourself and then playing it back while sitting back, closing your eyes and following the recorded instructions; [2] perhaps have a non-threatening friend [*not* the one whose relationship you are considering] read the script aloud to you; or [3] **making use of the spoken rendition of the Rope Trick mental imagery exercise *read aloud by the author* and that, at the time of publication of this book, has been posted on YouTube** at https://www.youtube. com/watch?v=bdXyfAbY4Ag . This rendition has been provided for the convenience of individuals who have read this book and are aware of the information and precautions provided herein, so that they may just sit back, close their eyes and follow the spoken instructions of the exercise. [Please note that this video may only be available on YouTube for a limited period of time after the publication of this book. You may access this 9:21 minute long video by either using the link above or going onto the YouTube website and searching for *"Cupchik Rope Trick"*]

The responsibility for making use of the contents of this book and/or the YouTube video is the informed user's alone, and only the user shall bear the responsibility for the imagery sequence produced by him or her, its interpretation and any consequences that might follow from its use. It is also strongly recommended that only persons who <u>are currently in treatment with an experienced counsellor or psychotherapist,</u> carry out this exercise.

[After inviting the individual to sit back in a chair or on a couch I prepare the client as follows:]

"The mental imagery exercise that we will be doing shortly will involve you imaging yourself being with someone with whom you have an important relationship in your current life, perhaps your spouse or lover, parent, sibling, child, in-law, co-worker or supervisor.

"Please take time now to decide which other person you will be considering in your imaging."

[**After a short pause of 10 or so seconds, the Rope Trick experience proper is introduced as follows:**]
"The exercise you will be given shortly is called a fantasy exercise. Fantasy exercises have been found to be useful as well as interesting ways of viewing ourselves.

"Shortly I shall be asking you to allow yourself to imagine, that is, to actually <u>imagine</u> or <u>picture</u> in front of your mind's eye, a scene. There's only one precaution for you to take in order to have this exercise work for you, and that is to allow yourself to actually let yourself see, in your imagination, what will be happening. This is different than trying to think about what <u>should</u> be happening, or even, what you would <u>like</u> to have happen. Don't worry about how to know whether the scene you will be viewing is the 'right' one or not. If you are <u>actually seeing</u>, that is, picturing the scene, rather than either thinking about the picture or computing it, then a relevant picture will just kind of 'pop' into your mind without you thinking about making it up.

"Some people find it helpful to imagine that they are looking at a sort of 'movie screen' in their heads, what we call a 'mind screen'; the picture then appears on it!

"You will have lots of time to have your fantasy; you won't be rushed; if you find that your fantasy doesn't appear immediately, don't be concerned; it may take a little time, but it will come if you allow it and don't try to <u>compute</u> it or <u>force</u> it, and you will have time to have your fantasy."

[Moderate relaxation phase:]
"Beginning now, and for the duration of the exercise, I would like you keep your eyes closed; I will let you know when to reopen them. Do now arrange your body so that you can find a position you will be comfortable staying in for a while. Now, would you attend even more to your body and to the sensations that you experience.
[Pause for 15 seconds]

"Become aware of any tension that you may have happening in your body **[pause for five seconds]**. *Beginning with your toes, and all the way up to the top of your head, gradually move your awareness* <u>along</u> *and* <u>up</u> *your body; anywhere that you find tension, allow yourself to tense yourself even more for a moment or two, then release the tension and relax that area and move on to the next area.*
[Provide about 30 seconds for this progressive relaxation sequence to happen]

"Now, begin attending to your breathing - your breathing in and breathing out. Now allow yourself to simply enjoy this more relaxed state of being for a while."
[Pause for about 30 seconds]

[The Rope Trick imaging exercise proper:]
"Now, would you let yourself imagine that you are somewhere that is not quite like any place you have ever been to, seen pictures of, or have had described to you before, and that you are there with that other person. Let yourself actually see <u>yourself</u>, *that* <u>other person</u>, *and a* <u>rope</u> *in the same picture.*

"The rope may or may not be near and/or making contact with either or both of you. The rope is made up of any material, any color, any diameter, any length, any strength; all its characteristics and all other aspects of the imagery will appear to you as you attend to your mind screen.

8

"Allow yourself to observe the images that appear on your mind screen as you would a movie. Let yourself <u>see</u> and possibly <u>hear</u> the action.

[Pause for about <u>two minutes</u> to allow time for the individual to have the fantasy exercise]

"Let the action continue until it comes to an ending. If it doesn't appear to have an ending, then attempt to make one happen.
[Pause for about 15 seconds.]

"If no ending comes, that is all right. Not everything has to have an ending on command."

[Imagery enhancement Phase:]
"Now, for the next few moments please make use of the memory-recording capacity of your mind and rerun segments of your imagery attending particularly to the following details; check out <u>whether</u> and <u>how</u> the rope <u>may have been close to and/or in contact with either one or both of you</u>. Please see, on your mind screen, what the <u>ends</u> of the rope look like. What is the <u>color</u>, <u>condition</u> and <u>kind</u> of rope that you had in your fantasy? Also allow yourself to rerun any other aspects of your imagery that you care to and when you've finished doing all of this, and you can take your time, simply relax with your hands on the arms of the chair or by your side."

[Recording the imagery:]
"Keeping your eyes closed, please rerun the imagery sequence on your 'mind screen' again and describe it out loud, in the present tense, as if it is happening now for the first time.

"Check out if there is anything that is part of the imagery that you did not notice before, and if there is, mention it now.

[The individual is then asked, after describing the imagery out loud, if it is being recorded or if a therapist is present, to write it

down, either longhand or at a computer keyboard. This concludes the formal rendering of the Rope Trick mental imagery exercise.]

****

Chapter 2

IMPORTANT THINGS TO NOTE WHEN USING THE ROPE TRICK EXERCISE

A Caveat: Not all exercises work equally well, or even at all, with *all* therapy clients *all* the time. I practice psychotherapy employing numerous creative techniques such as mental imagery, Gestalt therapy, two-chair work, systematic desensitization, and other modern approaches; most times these approaches work extremely well yet at other times they may fall somewhat flat. An analogy that most of us can relate to is the fact that there is seldom a single medication that works for all persons who have cases of somewhat similar or even exactly identical diseases.

Is it possible that the insightful experiences of the original group members who were present had when the Rope Trick was first created and presented, simply 'a fluke'?
Years of offering the Rope Trick have demonstrated that the imagery experiences or 'responses' that its users had were indeed meaningful to them and were not simply random, pointless productions.

The Rope Trick may be used over and over again by the same person, in regard to the same or different relationships at different times in order to perhaps gain new insights and information about the then-current nature of the relationships under consideration. As well, you and the person whose relationship you have used the Rope Trick to consider, can *each* use the Rope Trick *separately* and then review your imagery experiences together, preferably with the assistance of a relationship counselor. By so doing, perhaps you may acquire greater insight into how you view yourselves in relation to one another - and then, hopefully, if you need or want to, you may choose to change to better accommodate each others' needs and wants.

Be aware, however, that the preferable way of using the Rope Trick, at least initially, is to do so on your own. You and/or your partner might not be particularly pleased with what your respective Rope Trick responses appear to indicate, and unless you are both ready and willing to discuss your respective responses in a mutually supportive atmosphere, preferably with the assistance of an independent, suitably educated psychotherapist, the consequences could be quite disturbing.

In my own clinical practice I prefer to offer the Rope Trick to each member of a couple at separate times so that we can discuss their individual experiences without the other person being present, which usually allows for a more open and free discussion. Then, if both have indicated that they are ready and willing to share their experiences with one another, they might do so in a follow-up joint session.

Chapter 3

WHY THE ROPE TRICK WORKS AND HOW TO INTERPRET YOUR OWN RESPONSES TO THE EXERCISE

Let's now get into the nitty-gritty of how and why the Rope Trick exercise works. Do keep in mind that it required literally years of in-depth investigation to uncover the answers to these questions. What I intend to do in this chapter and the ones to follow is to present you with some of the *major* elements of what I have uncovered. I will also provide you with numerous composite examples of Rope Trick responses that a good many people have had.

It might be of interest to know that during the five years that it took to complete my doctoral dissertation, I was always at the ready [as is true of most graduate students] to make inquiries of nearly every person I encountered during that period who I thought might have an at least partial answer to one or more of the questions that I was attempting to resolve. And on a number of occasions my curiosity did, in fact, yield some very useful information.

As an example, when I was speaking with a professional actor about my interest in the subject of ropes, she excused herself and shortly afterward came back into the room carrying two books that she thought I would be interested in examining. And she was right! One of the books was called *A Dictionary Of Symbols* by J. E. Cirlot and, sure enough, listed in the dictionary was the word "rope" and that book provided very interesting notions about the possible symbolic meanings of ropes, including, of course, tying or binding two things together. The other book was called *To The Actor*, by Michael Chekhov. That book also spoke to the issue of imagery as well, and helped me further my understanding regarding why the Rope Trick might have the power that it had persistently displayed.

A crucial insight about ropes and relationships:
I challenge the reader to find an exception to the following statement [but if you do, kindly email me to wcupchik@aol.com]: for over 40 years I have wanted to be informed of such an exception - as of the writing of this book I am still waiting.

****

Every single word, phrase, term and expression that can be used to describe the *characteristics* and/or *functions* of a <u>rope</u> can also be used to describe the *characteristics* and/or *functions* of a <u>relationship</u> at any particular instant in time.
Take a moment now and challenge yourself to think of words, phrases and expressions that might be used to describe the characteristics and/or functions of a <u>rope</u>; write down your answers on the left-hand side of an otherwise blank page. Now, do the same in regard to the characteristics and/or functions of a <u>relationship</u> and write down those answers on the right-hand side of the same page. Have you found a single word or phrase or expression that applies to ropes but would not apply to a relationship, or vice versa? I doubt it, but if you have found such a case, then congratulations and *please*, do email me with your discovery.

The fact is, I believe, that *any* words that might be used to describe the <u>characteristics</u> of ropes and relationships are the same. For example:
- strong or weak,
- colorful or bland,
- long or short,
- flexible or rigid,
- new or old,
- frayed or shiny,
- rough or smooth,
- stationary or in motion,
- etc…

It may seem remarkable but experience with the Rope Trick exercise has shown that the words people use to describe <u>characteristics of the rope</u> that they saw in their imagery very often are also indicative of the current <u>characteristics of the relationship</u> they were considering. For instance, if the rope is described as strong or colorful or flexible or smooth or active, it usually turns out that the relationship under consideration also has those same positive qualities. On the other hand, if the rope imagined during the exercise was described as weak or rigid or frayed or stationary, that would often indicate negative aspects of the relationship between the two people [who in this book we will refer to as person A and person B].

****

Also, the words, phrases and expressions that can be used to describe the <u>functions</u> of ropes and relationships, are also the same. For example:

- tying the knot,
- being at loose ends,
- being tied up in knots,
- stringing someone along,
- handing someone a line,
- tugging at one's heartstring,
- cutting the cord,
- being given enough rope,
- feeling at loose ends,
- being tied up with someone,
- holding on by a thread,
… and so on.

I invite you, over the next several days, to pay attention to the phrases that your friends and/or the characters in a movie, play or novel that you may encounter, might use to describe their relationships. The above phrases are certainly common enough and very frequently used. Not surprisingly, in Rope Trick responses where the rope breaks or is seriously frayed, that usually suggests that those relationships are not in good shape at all.

15

****

Words and **phrases** describing the *ends* of the rope that may appear in a user's response and their possible parallel meanings vis-à-vis the relationship under consideration are also the very same: for example:

- tied in a knot,
- frayed,
- at loose ends,
- cleanly cut,
- smooth,
- rough,
- neatly bound;

… these and many other words may be used to describe one or both ends of the rope seen in individuals' mental imagery responses.

The condition of the end of the rope nearest the person who is carrying out the Rope Trick exercise is often indicative of the state of repair of his or her part of the relationship. In cases where the imager's end of the rope is in poor condition [perhaps frayed or unraveling], that person's attitude towards the relationship may be rather negative or lacking in commitment or involvement. On the other hand and/or at the same time, the imager may imagine that the *other* end of the rope, i.e. the end that may be closer to the other person, is somehow deficient. On occasion, this sort of image has occurred to people who may not have previously *consciously* viewed the other person as lacking in involvement or commitment to the relationship. However, once they view the rope in such a way, they may have a breakthrough into conscious awareness that all is not as positive as they had up to then considered it to be. Among the remarkable features of the Rope Trick is the fact that it may provide in the form of imagery, indications or suggestions that the imager may not have previously wanted to acknowledge. In other words, the Rope Trick sometimes overcomes or interrupts conscious denial of a possible negative aspect of the relationship that the imager had been avoiding.

****

Words and **Phrases** describing the *main portion* of the rope
that may appear in a user's response and their possible meanings:
- in good repair,
- colourful,
- worn out,
- bland,
- hanging loose,
- unattached,
- on the verge of breaking,
- having a number of knots along its length,
- on fire,
- all wet,
- shaking,
- soaked in blood, sweat and/or tears,

... are among the many words and phrases that have been
employed by users of the Rope Trick exercise to describe major
portions of the ropes they have viewed in their mental imagery
sequences. These words and phrases are also very often indicative of
the nature and qualities of the relationships under consideration.

It is always important to inquire into the qualities of the rope not
only at both ends but also in the middle as well. It sometimes happens
that the ends of the rope seem fine but an examination along the length
of the rope suggests a seriously damaged condition. Such a scenario
may happen in cases where both parties to the relationship are
essentially putting up a good front, so to speak, and not attending to
what is going on at the core of the relationship.

On the other hand, while one or both ends of the rope may appear
to be in a deteriorating condition, the main part of the rope may seem
very healthy indeed. Such imagery may indicate that the fundamentals
of the relationship are satisfactory but that there are one or more issues
with which one or both parties are currently having difficulty.

In any of the above scenarios, a closer examination of - and discussion about - issues that may be affecting the relationship, might well be in order.

****

<u>*Functions*</u> **of the rope in a particular user's response and their possible meanings:**

If only one person is holding on to the rope at any particular moment in time, that individual is likely to be the more invested in the relationship at that specific point.

If both parties are actively involved in holding onto the rope, e.g., moving or skipping with it, then the likelihood is that both parties are actively involved in the relationship.

Experience indicates that when the two individuals imagined in the sequence are holding onto the rope and playfully walking, running or skipping along in the same direction, their relationships are usually in a very positive state. Of course, it is possible that the imager is denying issues in the relationship and the Rope Trick experience may simply be reflecting that state of denial. Further consideration of the import of the imagery sequence is always worthwhile, whether the sequence has a positive, negative or neutral tint to it.

****

<u>If the two people are facing one another and touching and if the rope is wrapped tightly around them,</u> then the interpretation can be more difficult. Perhaps the rope is warmly embracing the two persons *or* they may be entangled with one another and are possibly having difficulty separating.

Consider <u>how the rope is being held or used</u> during the imagery sequence. Also the state of its activity or inactivity is worthwhile reviewing. Keep in mind that the rope itself, its characteristics, functions and behavior during the imagery sequence often speaks to the current nature of the relationship.

- In cases where the rope is simply <u>laying on the ground or on the sand and is not touching either of the two people</u>, it may be that the relationship is currently [at least in the imager's mind] in a state of passivity or stagnation.
- Experience shows that <u>whoever is closest to the rope is frequently the individual who is inclined to be the more involved</u> in the relationship at the moment.
- If the other person is viewed as <u>not even holding the rope</u>, that may indicate a current relative lack of involvement by that other person.
- When the rope appears to be playfully active, that is often an indication of a healthy relationship.
- If the rope is being whipped about rather violently, then perhaps not so much!

If the rope is being used as a weapon [as a whip or a noose, for example], that may suggest that the person using it in such a fashion is feeling very angry and/or vengeful towards the other person at that moment. My experience is that the use of a rope as a weapon within the imagery sequence <u>does not necessarily mean</u> that the imager is harboring potentially dangerous feelings or intentions towards the other person. However, such imagery does suggest that the individual might consider discussing his feelings towards the other person with that individual and/or an experienced mental health professional.

When the rope is <u>being used in a playful manner,</u> that may indicate that the two people are currently experiencing pleasure in their relationship, or at least pretending to do so.

When one person [person A] appears to be <u>employing the rope to assist the other individual</u> [person B], perhaps up a steep slope or difficult point in a climb or travel, that may suggest that A is currently in the more secure position [financially or otherwise] and/or is functioning as a caretaker of B.

If one person is seen as <u>suddenly letting go of - or cutting - the rope</u> that the other person is hanging onto, perhaps the former is currently backing away from involvement in some aspect of the relationship. For example, if person A, who has been considering entering into a business or intimate arrangement with person B, is seen as letting go of the rope in some fashion, then A may currently be inclined to back away from pursuing such an arrangement.

When one person is seen as <u>offering the rope to the other person,</u> then possibly the former is seeking a closer involvement with the other.

On the other hand, <u>if neither person is touching the rope</u> and it is perhaps merely laying on the ground, then the likelihood is that neither party is actively involved in, or willing to become more involved in, the relationship at that moment.

****

Scenes that may appear in a user's response and their possible meanings:

While it is true that virtually no two Rope Trick mental imagery experiences, among the many hundreds that have been shared with me, have been exactly the same, there have been, of course, some aspects that they have had in common. For example, the <u>settings</u> or <u>surroundings</u> of some of the responses have sometimes been similar. Among the settings that have presented themselves in various individuals' imagery responses have been <u>deserts</u>, <u>jungles</u>, <u>beaches</u>, <u>hills</u>, <u>mountains</u>, <u>solitary - or groups of - dwellings</u>, and <u>different bodies of water</u>, including <u>streams</u>, <u>waterfalls</u>, <u>rivers</u>, <u>lakes</u>, and <u>oceans</u>. Lets consider some of these in detail, as derived from examinations of different peoples' actual responses:

****

Deserts are usually *not* a very good sign of the current state of an interpersonal relationship. The sparseness of vegetation and absence of life-sustaining water often appears to indicate a lack of nourishment, energy or vibrancy in the relationship, at least from the Rope Trick user's perspective.

Several imagers have described the deserts they imagined as being quite indicative of the then state of their relationships with the other persons. Naturally, all relationships need nurturance and the lack of water or vegetation may suggest that the relationship is in serious need of same.

****

Jungles, on the other hand, are often indicative of the relationships' current state as being one of richness, excitement, adventure, and/or potential danger or at least, unpredictability.

While some imagers have described such settings as exciting, vibrant and a sensory feast, others have expressed a sense of foreboding and uncertainty when their Rope Trick experiences have been set in jungles.

****

Beaches, as long as they are relatively serene with waters gently lapping onto the shore, may suggest that the relationships are currently rather peaceful, relaxed and warm. If the waters are very rough and/or waves are crashing onto the shore, then perhaps not so much!

One of the more common settings for Rope Trick experiences has been a beach. It is always interesting to note how the imager [remember, we'll always refer to the imager as 'person A'] describes what the two individuals are doing during the sequence; in the scene, are they walking towards, parallel to, or away from the waters edge and/or each other? Which of the two individuals is walking closest to the water? What is the length, kind and condition of the rope? Are both persons in contact with the rope or is only one person [and which one?] touching or holding the rope and/or is it perhaps dragging behind? Or, is the rope laying on the sand? What have they been doing and/or what are they now doing with the rope? All of these questions may provide important clues as to the current state of the relationship that person A has with person B, at least from person A's perspective .

Familiarity with Rope Trick mental imagery exercise responses indicates, for example, that:
- Whoever is closest to the water may be the more involved in the relationship at the moment;
- If A and B are walking along parallel to the beach, possibly holding the rope playfully in their hands, that suggests that the relationship is currently fun and has good energy; *but*
- If only one person is holding onto the rope as it is being dragged along the sand behind him or her, the other person may be rather detached from the relationship;
- If the beach has lovely sand and swaying palm trees, that may be a positive sign for the relationship.

****

Other Bodies of water [streams, rivers, lakes, waterfalls, oceans] viewed in the Rope Trick mental imagery responses can be calm and serene, turbulent or perhaps even downright dangerous; the state of the relationship may be perceived as likewise.

If the imager sees either or both of the two people moving rapidly towards the brink of Niagara Falls, for instance, it may be that person A is consciously or at least intuitively aware that the relationship is approaching a very serious, possibly dangerous and perhaps even terminal situation.

****

Hills may be gently rolling and easy to climb or very craggy and difficult to traverse. As is true of most of the terrains that Rope Trick users may see in their imagery, the nature of the terrain might be suggestive of the kind and degree of difficulty or ease in the current state of their relationships.

Mountains, of course, may be of virtually any shape or size, and the responses may indicate that one or both persons are stationary, moving upwards or down, and having an easy or difficult time with the terrain. They may be on the surface -or even on the inside- of a mountain. It is easy to imagine that the rope may be being used to assist the other person.

It is interesting to consider that in both real mountain climbing and the climbing of sheer rock faces, an actual rope, of course, virtually always plays a vital part. If person A imagines that he or she is climbing a near-vertical rock face with person B, a rope will almost certainly be present. In such a real-life situation the kind and condition of the rope may play a key part in the eventual success or failure of the climb. Many of us have seen films, either fictional [think of the movie, *The Eiger Sanction*, for example] or of the National Geographic kind [think perhaps of the two young men, Tommy Caldwell and Kevin Jorgesen who, in early 2015, successfully free-climbed El Capitan's 'Dawn Wall' in Yosemite National Park]. In such circumstances it is clear that if one of the climbers slipped and fell, his life may truly have depended upon the rope and to what or whom it was connected.

****

A solitary dwelling may be seen within the imagery sequence, with two persons who may be either outside - or inside – of the structure and the qualities of the edifice [building materials, state of repair, etc…] may vary considerably. These factors may also be suggestive of aspects of the status and/or dynamics of the relationship.

Houses as well as ropes tend to hold great symbolic significance when it comes to individuals and their relationships. When a house is seen as being in good repair and of reasonable size, then just as when a rope is seen as being reasonably substantial and in good repair, it often indicates that the relationship being considered is likely to be in a healthy state. If a house and/or rope is seen as overly worn and/or in bad shape, that may also speak volumes.

****

A group of dwellings may be seen as part of the user's response.

Their nature may also inform upon the current status and dynamics of the relationship. If the buildings have been imagined to be inside a fortress-like wall, perhaps with the imaginer and the other person on different sides of the wall, that might suggest that there is currently a great deal of defensiveness and/or conflict happening in the relationship.

****

As should be clear from the above [non-totally inclusive] listing, *all* aspects of the imagery sequence may inform the user about how he or she really currently views the relationship.

****

The *activities* and *emotional tones* of the persons within the scenario are also, of course, important.

The persons viewed in the mental imagery scenario may be having an enjoyable or pleasant or difficult or downright awful time. They may be playful, laughing, arguing, fighting or ignoring each other, just as in the 'real' world.

****

The *activities* of the persons in the mental imagery scenario can inform about the status and dynamics of the relationship.

You may recall that the very first person for whom I created the Rope Trick exercise imagined herself trudging up a knee-deep snow covered hill with a very heavy rope slung over her shoulder and pulling her husband along behind her while he acted rather like a dead weight. That image was certainly worth several thousand words as it spoke to her about what, from her vantage point, was the unfair energy distribution that they each were contributing [or not] to their supposedly joint efforts.

****

Essentially, all *activities* seen in the Rope Trick responses can inform about the relationships they relate to, including whether:

- The two people are <u>moving along in the same direction</u>, sharing holding onto the rope; this is possibly a very good sign of mutual cooperation.

- The two persons, A and B, are <u>pulling on the rope in opposite directions</u>, as in a tug-of-war; they might be involved in a battle for control of one or more aspects of the relationship. Of course, it is preferable that the two individuals come to a mutually satisfactory means of resolving a control or conflict issue.

- A and B are <u>moving at right angles to one another</u>, i.e., moving further and further apart; perhaps indicative of lessened involvement or connection with one another.

It is an unfortunate aspect of some long-term relationships and marriages that while one of the two parties is growing intellectually, educationally, physically, creatively and/or spiritually, the other may not be moving in a compatible direction. Unfortunately, unless the person who is being 'left behind' begins to advance in a to-some-extent compatible direction, the relationship may eventually deteriorate or even come to an end. Alternately, the one who has been growing may experience increasing pressure to cease to do so.

****

<u>A and B are standing still</u>; so may be the relationship – or not!

Perhaps A and B are staring lovingly into each other's eyes while holding hands - very likely a positive scenario. Or, perhaps the two individuals are standing one or 2 feet apart, facing one another, each with his or her arms crossed in front of their respective chests and with scowls on their faces. Each aspect of the Rope Trick mental imagery response that an individual has may offer important clues as to the current state of the relationship so it is important not to rely on merely one or two elements of the imagery sequence.

****

A and/or B are sinking in quicksand; possibly a very poor sign as to how the relationship is doing, at least as far as the person whose Rope Trick response it is, is concerned.

A and B are laying down together on a beach, holding each other and/or making love; possibly a very positive sign indeed.

B is tying up A with a strong, tightly wound rope; this may indicate that A is feeling very restricted by, threatened by, or insecure regarding B at this time.

The interpretation of the state of the relationship by simply noting the activities of the two persons involved is frequently almost self-explanatory, especially if viewed as directly symbolic of how the person whose Rope Trick response it is, views the relationship at the time the mental imagery exercise was done.

Please note: Do keep in mind that the Rope Trick is a *'here and now'* exercise; it can only offer a *symbolic* representation of the relationship at the moment that the mental imagery exercise is done. If the two parties have just had a strong disagreement but get past that troublesome issue, say in an hour or so, and then 'make up', then the individual's Rope Trick responses will be quite different from one another if done at the 'before' and 'after' points.

Chapter 4

TWO PEOPLE DON'T HAVE ONLY ONE RELATIONSHIP

Imagine, if you will, the following conversation between two persons in an intimate relationship:

Person A: *"We need to talk. I think our relationship is in trouble."*
Person B: *"I don't know what you are talking about. I think our relationship is fine."*
Person A: *"Well it's not!"*
Person B: *"Well I think you're wrong."*
Person A: *"I am not wrong! Our relationship is not working."*
Person B: *"Our relationship is working great so what you're saying doesn't make sense to me."*

And around and around that they go, stale-mated [literally and figuratively] from the get-go. It is very easy for one person to stonewall another by simply denying that there is a problem in "our" *relationship* [singular].

The very common problem couples face when dealing with issues that they have with one another is that they talk about "our" relationship. Too frequently the counselors or therapists from whom they seek help also tend to speak with person A and person B about "*your* relationship [singular]", as if there is only one relationship to be spoken about. The fact is that the use of such language often inhibits any thorough resolution because, while person A may say, "I am not satisfied with *our* relationship", person B may well reply, "I don't know what you are talking about; *our* relationship is fine as far as I am concerned." And if their therapist [if they have one] doesn't correct them, then they may indeed stay stuck, at least, perhaps, until one of them relents.

I suggest that the problem here is that person A's relationship with person B is one relationship [and person A may or may not be satisfied with it] while person B's relationship with person A is

actually a different relationship [and person B may or may not be satisfied with his or her relationship with person A].

In fact, this is very often the situation that brings at least one member of a couple to a therapist's office most reluctantly, perhaps because he or she is genuinely confused as to what the problem is, since that person doesn't see one, or at least not the same one as the person who is pressing for some re-solution.

One of the very first steps, then, is to educate the two members of a couple to the fact that each of them has a relationship with the other that is idiosyncratic; in other words, each of us has our own perspective and responses to the relationship that we have with another person. One of the easiest and quickest ways to help shed some light on whatever the issues may be, is to have each person "own" the relationship that he or she has the other person. **This can most easily be accomplished by using phrases such as, "I am not satisfied in *my* relationship with you although I appreciate that you may be satisfied with *your* relationship with me."**

As an example, if one member of a couple [say person B] tends to be extremely controlling and has been so for, let us suppose, the first several years of the marriage, the controlling person who has basically dictated what they both did together and when, [such as which movies they went to; what they had for meals and where, what their respective responsibilities around the home were, etc...], the other member [person A] may, sooner or later, get fed up with being controlled and might wish to set new rules and/or roles, change their respective responsibilities and have much more say about the choices that are made. It is often true that the individual who is exercising the greater control over the activities of a couple tends to be the more comfortable with the current situation because whatever he or she wants to get or do, the couple gets and does.

[An interesting example of a variation on this scenario displayed itself while I was on the psychology staff at the Clarke Institute of

Psychiatry, in Toronto. The powers that were decided that it would be a healthy matter if representatives of each discipline, i.e., psychiatry, psychology, social work, nursing, physiotherapy and occupational therapy, were to meet together regularly and discuss issues of mutual concern in their relationships with one another. Although this situation happened more than three decades ago I well remember that the psychiatrist-member of the group expressed his astonishment when he heard some members of the other disciplines utter their concerns about the degree to which psychiatrists effectively dictated how the Institute was run. The psychiatrist, as I recall a young chap relatively new to the profession and the Institute, exclaimed, "Gosh, I sure don't feel a difference between us when it comes to issues of control." At that point one of the other members of the group exclaimed, "Well that's because you have control. It's those of us who don't have much control that are only too aware of the fact that we don't."]

Among the 40 subjects who took part in the experimental phase of my doctoral dissertation were four couples. In other words, eight of the 40 subjects to whom I gave the mental imagery exercise were 'paired'. I still well recall my initial astonishment when looking at the results of the filled out Relationship Questionnaires for the pairs, when I discovered that while one member of a couple [say person A] scored the relationship that he or she had with person B as 'very highly adequate', the other member of the couple, person B, had rated the relationship that he or she had with person A very differently in terms of adequacy of their respective relationships.

Not surprisingly, the nature of the Rope Trick responses that the two members of a couple have are often markedly different. Whereas one member of a couple may have produced an imagery experience that was quite benign or even positive, the other member of the same couple may have provided a markedly different kind of Rope Trick response, one that was not at all pleasant.

To summarize then, keep in mind that:
No two people [A and B] necessarily have similar needs or wants from the relationships they have with one another.

Or perhaps *they do* have the same or similar needs [e.g., both like to be 'looked after' -in colloquial terms, both are 'takers'- but don't like to do the 'looking after' –i.e., neither are 'givers'] and that would possibly not make for a satisfying experience for one, or both.

As another example, person A may have a high sexual drive and likes to have sexual relations relatively often, while person B has the opposite inclination. This can be a major issue for some couples, one that requires negotiation, and as likely as not, some accommodation. Furthermore, individuals' needs and/or wants for sexual activity may change over the years and a recognition of the need for a new discussion in this regard may be required.

[As for this particular area of an intimate relationship, I am reminded of the insightful if somewhat simplistic comment of a New York City psychologist, offered during a conversation that several of us professionals were having on the terrace of the Gouldings' *Western Institute for Group and Family Therapy* near Watsonville, California in 1972; she said almost matter-of-factly, *"You know, if the sex is good in the relationship it represents about 3% of the relationship. However, if the sex is not satisfactory, it then accounts for about 97% of the relationship."*

****

Developing the *Cupchik Relationship Questionnaire*© and offering it to both members of a couple - at different times.
In order to carry out a rigorous experimental investigation of the validity and reliability of the Rope Trick for purposes of my thesis, I was required to find a pen-and-paper device that would allow the 40 subjects to rate the adequacy of their relationships and for three psychologist-raters [the latter, of different theoretical orientations] to rate the written responses of the subjects to the Rope Trick exercise as

a means of quantifying the *apparent* satisfactoriness of their relationships. Since a thorough investigation of then available relationship-related tools failed to provide a satisfactory option, I was required to create a new 'relationship questionnaire' that would be compatible with the qualities of the Rope Trick responses. The result of this effort was the 24 item, multiple-choice *Cupchik Relationship Questionnaire©*.

In other words, from the verbal [and then transcribed] responses that each of the 40 individuals had provided after carrying out the Rope Trick exercise, each of the three psychologists rated the relationship described by a subject via his or her Rope Trick response in terms of four mutually exclusive factors that I labelled *emotional warmth*, *mutual dependency*, *balance of control*, and the [lack of] *malice.*

I have virtually always offered the Relationship Questionnaire to each member of a couple during one of their individual sessions, at which time we have gone over the ratings of the relationship in detail. Then, with their permissions, at a later time we examined the results of their Relationship Questionnaires with the two members of the couple together in my office at the same time. It has usually been very instructive for each person to realize that his or her partner may have a very different view of their relationships generally, and perhaps even of the same issue [emotional warmth, malice, etc...] in particular. For example, person A may have indicated that there was no sense of malice in the relationship while person B had a quite different view.

Not infrequently, the person [say, person B] who had not perceived that the partner [person A] believed there to be a degree of malice emanating from B, has been shocked to learn that the partner viewed things so very differently. What frequently followed was a detailed discussion of why person A believed there to be an issue of malice. Perhaps this sense of malice stemmed from the partner's [B's] harsh tone of voice, use of foul language and/or talk of separation or divorce whenever major issues arose between them. It also may be that person B had not realized just how upsetting this was to the partner [A]. The response of the offender has sometimes been along the lines of, "Don't you realize that when I'm upset that's just how I speak but that I don't mean you to take me seriously?"

As Marshall McLuhan once said, "A message isn't a message until it gets read," and he might very well have elaborated, stating that, "The message *received* may not have been the same as that that the messenger may have *intended* to deliver". A thorough discussion of the ways in which each member of a couple rated their relationships with one another has almost invariably produced some valuable insights and, sometimes as well, an improvement in some aspects of their communications. At the least, previously unrecognized perceived differences have been brought to the surface.

Chapter 5

ILLUSTRATIVE EXAMPLES OF ROPE TRICK RESPONSES

Let's consider some actual [but composite and camouflaged] Rope Trick responses in some detail.

While the variety of mental imagery experiences that people may have when carrying out the Rope Trick mental imagery exercise is virtually infinite, it can be instructive to consider a few intriguing examples in detail. The reader will then be in a more informed position from which to consider his [or her client's] Rope Trick experience.

****

CASE # 1: LYNDA, THE FIRST EVER USER OF THE ROPE TRICK MENTAL IMAGERY EXERCISE.

This case has been mentioned previously. Lynda saw herself trudging up a long, sharp incline, knee deep in snow, while at the same time tugging on a long, thick rope that was slung heavily over her shoulder and extended all the way back to her husband who was about 20 feet behind her, where the rope was tied around his waist in a knot. She was doing almost all the work, pulling him along as she advanced up the steep hill.

Re the <u>characteristics and functions of the rope</u> in Lynda's response:

- The rope was <u>very heavy,</u> and Lynda had to literally and symbolically pull not only her own weight but that of her husband, as he was not helping get up the hill by contributing any significant effort of his own;

- The rope was <u>long,</u> as had been their marital relationship;

- The rope was <u>tied around his waist, at nearly the belly button position,</u> and she indeed considered herself to be the only adult present; her husband was acting more like a dependent, helpless child, with the rope being in proximity to where his umbilical cord had been. She described her husband as having been very passive throughout the last few years of their marriage, and…

- <u>She was getting exhausted</u> by having to do most of the 'heavy lifting' in their marriage.

Re the <u>surroundings</u>:
- A <u>very wintery scene</u>: cold, deep snow on a steep incline, making movement very difficult. Lynda explained when discussing her Rope Trick response, that things were indeed very difficult in their lives at the time and there had been a definite 'chill' in their relationship for an extended period.

- In fact, they were experiencing serious financial stresses at the time [hence the steep incline?] as Lynda's husband had lost his job many months earlier and seemingly [at least as far as Lynda could determine] he was not putting much effort into finding new employment.

Re the <u>relative positioning and movement</u> of the two persons:
- Although they were both moving in the same direction [*up* the hill], her husband was acting as a near 'dead weight', thereby making it exceedingly difficult for Lynda to move forward. This clearly reflected the absence of both persons working together, with each of them literally pulling their own weight.

<u>The Takeaway</u>:
Once she had carried out the Rope Trick exercise Lynda gained immediate insight into the then-current nature of her unsatisfactory and lopsided relationship with her husband. Until she had done the exercise it appears that she had avoided the obvious, probably due to the repercussions that were likely to have to follow; specifically, either

she would have to engage her highly defensive husband in drastically altering his passive, emotionally draining ways in his relationship with her, or perhaps, if he continued in the same manner, she would likely consider leaving their marriage.

****

CASE # 2: MARY AND THE NOOSE.

Let's now consider another striking case in some detail, that of Mary, the woman who imagined that she and her husband were in a desert-like environment close to a lone, leafless, dead tree, and that she was holding both ends of a sturdy but worn rope, where one end was tied in the form of a noose, and she had imagined herself looking for a strong branch over which she could toss the noose-end so that she could hang her husband. Her husband was entirely passive in the scene, waiting for Mary to act. Mary was very disturbed by the imagery experience and reported that she had repeatedly tried to change it to a different, or at least more benign, imagery – *but it kept returning*!

Regarding the <u>characteristics</u> and <u>functions</u> of the rope in Mary's response:
- Now, the fact that she imagined the particular sequence she did, did not *necessarily* mean, of course, that she *literally* wanted to hang [or in some other way, actually kill or even physically harm] her husband. Rather, the particular rope she saw, and what she imagined herself doing with it, possibly more likely symbolized that, at that moment, she was very angry -indeed furious- with her husband. She told me that she kept trying to change the imagery into a "nicer" one but the same image kept returning, seemingly spontaneously, perhaps suggesting that Mary's aggressive feelings towards her husband were very strong though still quite unacceptable to her.

• The fact that Mary was holding both ends of the rope suggests that she had, perhaps, taken control of her relationship and that what she planned to do next, specifically to toss the noose end of the rope over a branch, may well indicate that she meant to end the relationship, possibly in an aggressive, or at least, very assertive way. Taking definitive action by filing for divorce would be an example of such an action.

• On the other hand, keeping in mind that the Rope Trick mental imagery exercise is a here-and-now device, Mary's imagery sequence might have merely indicated some temporary but very major frustration with her husband.

Regarding the <u>surroundings</u>:
• The fact that the scene was a desolate one [in fact, a desert] may suggest a lack of nourishment for Mary in her relationship. There was no indication of anything growing in the scene; the tree is the only former living thing present, but it was currently lifeless and leafless.

Regarding the <u>relative positioning and movement of the two persons</u>:
• Mary is the only active figure in the scene. Her husband is entirely passive, seemingly awaiting his fate. He is neither running away nor taking any action to change Mary's mind in regard to what she is about to do. Indeed, this imagery does seem to reflect what was actually happening in Mary's life, as she later told me that she was intending to see a divorce lawyer within a week, that her husband knew of her intention and, for whatever reasons, had not attempted to talk her out of it.

The Takeaway:

Once she had carried out the Rope Trick exercise Mary said that she actually felt better, perhaps since her unconscious had evidently finally found a way to break through to her conscious mind and reflect the notion that she and her husband were in dire straits. She had now recognized the fact through imagery and had found a way to release some of her pent up resentments towards her husband. The fact that Mary kept trying to change the imagery indicates that she was very uncomfortable with the symbolized degree of her fury. That the same image kept returning suggests that her very angry feelings towards her husband refused to be denied.

****

CASE # 3: DAVID AND THE SWINGING ROPE.

David's Rope Trick experience was a very positive one. He imagined himself and his wife of 5 years walking along a warm Caribbean beach, each holding one end of a five-foot long, very colourful, strong but light rope. They were swinging the rope back and forth as they might a small child and were happily chatting with one another while enjoying the warm sand and beautiful aqua-green color of the ocean.

Regarding the characteristics and functions of the rope in David's response:

- The rope was colourful, as was the marriage of these two high performing professionals. They were very active in their community both as individuals and as a 'power couple'.

- The rope happened to be five feet long and they had been married for five years. *On occasion [experience suggests about 15% to 20% of the time, in fact] the length of the rope, in feet, approximately corresponds to the length of the relationship, in years. This co-incidence may be considered merely a curious chance correlation only, but has been observed enough times to make it worthy of comment. To date*

I have no indication as to how folks who use the metric system would respond, length-wise.

- The rope was being used in a playful manner, the couple swinging it back and forth as they might swing a young child whose hands they were holding, between them. Interestingly, David later commented that they had recently decided to have a child, as they both were experiencing parental urges and the time seemed right; they had recently purchased a house in the suburbs with a back yard that happened to have a swing and that they had decided could easily hold a child's playhouse and shallow wading pool.

Regarding the <u>surroundings</u>:
- The setting was that of a warm Caribbean beach. Such beaches often have gentle wave action with safe, refined sand and ample, varied and colourful vegetation on the landward side.

- The setting suggests a very fertile, colourful, peaceful and nourishing environment, which was the way that David described his happy marriage during our discussion following his mental imagery experience.

Regarding the <u>relative positioning and movement of the two persons</u>:
- David and his wife were walking side by side, moving along in unison and with pleasure. They were sufficiently close that the rope was not being held rigidly, yet they were able to easily play with the rope by swinging it backwards and forwards in unison.

- In fact, David considered himself and his wife as being very much at the same contented place vis-à-vis their marriage and their readiness and desire to have children.

The <u>Takeaway</u>:

Having carried out the Rope Trick mental imagery exercise, David stated that he felt even greater warmth towards his wife, and said that he had moved even closer towards his readiness and desire to have a child.

****

CASE # 4: BILL: A MOST DELICATE ROPE TRICK EXAMPLE: ONE END OF THE ROPE WAS TIED AROUND HIS Ph.D. SUPERVISOR'S 'PRIVATE PARTS'

A decidedly different example of the Rope Trick mental imagery exercise was provided to me by Bill, a Ph.D. graduate student. His thesis supervisor, Harry, was the chair of the department of economics in which he was pursuing his studies. Bill reported that Harry evidently believed that his own brand of economic theory was suitable for virtually *everyone* and *all societies* at *all times* and *under all conditions*, and that no other kind of economic theory was ever likely to be needed by anyone else in the field. As was the case with most of the other professors in the department, Bill did not entirely share his supervisor's *total* enthusiasm for his economic theory.

This graduate student told me that when he did the Rope Trick with his supervisor in mind, a rather embarrassing imagery experience immediately occurred to him. In this imagined scene he saw himself climbing a very steep, bare rock-faced mountain, one that was substantially higher than the adjacent mountain on which his supervisor was standing, and that the long, strong but light rope that he [the graduate student] was holding one end of, was actually hanging over a crag high above him and extended over to another outcropping on the adjacent mountain at a somewhat higher altitude, and then extended downwards to where his supervisor was standing, also at a higher altitude than was Bill. While Bill held his end of the rope rather gingerly in his hands as he climbed higher up the mountain he was on, the other end of the rope was seen as clearly tied around his supervisor's genitalia while Harry was standing still.

Bill said that when he had the imagery experience he inwardly laughed as he believed that he instantly recognized the meaning of his Rope Trick experience. He said he believed that his future would possibly carry him much higher in the field of economics then his supervisor was likely to ever achieve [a not unusual attitude for a Ph.D. candidate to have], but that he also was well aware, at the moment, that he needed his supervisor's help and blessing to be successful in the program.

In other words, the graduate student's mountain was much taller than his supervisor's but at the moment Bill was very much dependent upon Harry's assistance and support as he climbed higher and higher up his own mountain. The fact that he saw the other end of the rope tied around his thesis supervisor's genitalia symbolized for him that he needed to be very careful as he held onto the rope, in order to climb higher up his own mountain while at the same time, doing so in a manner that would not hurt, damage or upset his supervisor's very sensitive ego, macho mentality and rather rigid academic mind.

Regarding the <u>characteristics and functions</u> of the rope in Bill's response:

- The rope was described as "long, strong but light", which tends to correspond to the kind of connection that Ph.D. students typically have with their supervisors: such an academic relationship may be expected to last for a considerable period of time, perhaps up to four or five years or even longer;

- The Ph.D. candidate/supervisor relationships often develop strong personal, as well as academic, elements; the rope was clearly very strong and long but of limited length.

- The student/supervisor relationship may be 'heavy' or 'light' at the Ph.D. level. The fact that Bill knew it would take him years to complete his doctoral work made it important, he believed, to keep the relationship with his supervisor as 'light' as possible, while retaining the strength that would be required to complete his own complicated yet apparently very original thesis.

Regarding the <u>surroundings</u> in Bill's response:
- It is probably highly symbolic that Bill saw himself and his supervisor on adjacent mountains. Climbing a mountain is often considered symbolic of the act of attaining an achievement, according to many researchers in symbolism.

- While one end of the rope was in Bill's hands, the other end was tied around his supervisor's genitals and the surroundings [two adjacent mountains] were inherently potentially dangerous; his particular imagery might well suggest that Bill considered his supervisor to be threatened by his own potential. Whether that view was valid or not was not as important [as was stated above, many graduate students see themselves as perhaps eventually outdoing their supervisors in achievement] as the fact is that Bill believed that his supervisor's 'academic manhood' was potentially being threatened by him and therefore it was important that he not endanger - or appear to jeopardize - it.

Regarding the <u>relative positioning and movement of the two persons</u>:
- While Bill saw his mountain as being higher than that of his supervisor, suggesting perhaps that he considered himself as eventually being capable of greater academic achievement than his supervisor, at the same time he was keenly aware that the academic 'height' he had achieved to this point in time was still below that of his supervisor.

- In the imagery Bill saw himself as climbing higher while he saw his supervisor as stationary, suggesting that he thought Harry was likely to remain at the level of professional development and accomplishment he had already achieved.

The Takeaway:

Until he had carried out the Rope Trick mental imagery exercise Bill had not consciously acknowledged to himself just how very threatened his supervisor might be by his academic potential. Having a clearer sense that this might be the case, Bill determined to be particularly careful, when discussing differing views with his supervisor, to not demean or diminish the latter's opinions, but rather to *very gently* present his own, often alternate views, an approach that required considerable conscious restraint on Bill's part.

Bill later reported to me that his new, more deliberate approach to handling discussions with his supervisor was already yielding positive results. His supervisor had even put forward some of Bill's ideas at faculty meetings as really being highly compatible with his own. [P.S., Bill received his Ph.D. two years later, with his supervisor's full blessing. Bill credited the insights he had gained via the Rope Trick as having played a not insignificant part in assisting him to acquire his doctorate with maximum support and minimal opposition from his supervisor.]

****

CASE # 5: WAYNE, A PASSIVE, UNASSERTIVE PARTNER.

Wayne was a highly intelligent, mild-mannered professional whose relationship with his live-in common-law partner had been going steadily downhill, in his estimation, during the previous two years of their decade-long living together. However, he was not sure why that was the case, since as far as he was concerned they were still in love with each other.

Wayne's Rope Trick mental response revealed some likely serious problems in his relationship with his partner. In his imagery he saw her holding one end of a yo-yo and then realized that at the other end of the yo-yo was a miniature version of himself. The cord of the yo-yo was tied around his middle and his partner was playing with the 'toy', twirling him around in the fashion that experienced yo-yo users can easily do. The rope itself was about 4-1/2 feet in length and sufficiently strong to carry out its function and his partner was having no difficulty playing with it [him?] at her leisure.

Regarding the characteristics and functions of the rope in Wayne's response:

- The rope in Wayne's imagery sequence had one end tied into a knot around a miniaturized version of himself at his middle while his partner's finger was inserted into the loop at the other end. She was actively playing with the 'yo-yo' and as a result, Wayne was being moved up and down and round and round, continually twirled about his axis just like the wooden part of a yo-yo might be. He was feeling entirely out of control, dizzy and nauseous. The rope also kept occasionally getting twisted along its length. While his partner and the yo-yo seemed to be regular-sized, he appeared to be only a few inches in length and easily suspended at the end of the yo-yo.

- Wayne was initially quite embarrassed as he related his imagery sequence. The fact that he seemed so small and almost insignificant relative to his partner, and that she was, at least figuratively, twisting him about her finger, and that he was helpless to alter how she was dealing with him, were particularly disturbing features of the imagery. Within a few minutes, however, Wayne acknowledged that his partner did indeed seem to be almost entirely in control of their relationship – especially in terms of *when* they did *what* and *where* as far as their spending, home and social activities were concerned.

Regarding the <u>surroundings</u> in Wayne's response:

- Wayne did not provide any indication of the surroundings in which the action was taking place. The lack of context may also have been indicative of the state of their relationship; he appeared to have lost his way – and himself - in this relationship and was rather 'lost in [otherwise empty] space'.

Regarding the <u>relative positioning and movement of the two persons</u>:

- Most definitely, Wayne was in an entirely controlled position in the imagery. He was clearly overpowered and was being moved about at his partner's whim. She was essentially holding her ground while he was being moved about in all directions by her actions.

The <u>Takeaway</u>:

Wayne realized that his passivity and 'smallness' had been familiar positions for him in previous intimate relationships as well. The graphic illustration of his pattern that was so readily revealed by his Rope Trick response prompted him to ask to be referred to a therapist for his personal growth in general, and for assertiveness training in particular.

****

The five examples of Rope Trick responses above are indicative of the wide variety of mental imagery experiences that clients and workshop participants may have. You may wish to keep a notebook or file of your own Rope Trick experiences that you might accumulate over time. If you were to carry out the exercise over a period of several years in regard to the same or different 'other persons', it could be very illuminating to review how the Rope Trick responses might have changed over time. To the extent that the takeaways may remain very similar, that also may be worthwhile knowing.

Chapter 6

COULD SOMEONE DELIBERATELY DISTORT A RESPONSE TO THE ROPE TRICK?

The possibility of deliberately and consciously manipulating or altering the Rope Trick response that one produces.

Well, you might ask, "Alright, Dr Cupchik, I am willing to consider the possibility that the exercise you call the Rope Trick produces some interesting imagery scenarios, but couldn't I simply *make* the Rope Trick imagery sequence turn out the way I might *want* it to be rather than the way it actually *is*?

Let me respond to that question in the following ways:

A highly defended person *might* be able to produce an, in some ways, misleading Rope Trick response, although I am not aware of a single instance when this has happened, precisely because the imagery emerges from the unconscious and is therefore not very accessible to conscious or deliberate distortion. Nevertheless, it must be allowed that such a distorted, highly defended imagery sequence *might* be capable of being produced. *Let the user beware.*

Over time it usually becomes easier for a user of the Rope Trick who is honest with himself to recognize whether his unconscious and/or subconscious have attempted to alter his response as a means of self-deception.

There is, moreover, a powerful reason to consider that the response produced by a user of the Rope Trick likely does has some validity. Consider the following statement from the writings of the famous psychiatrist Carl Jung, [from *The Collected Works of C.G. Jung, Vol. 18, The Symbolic Life, 1975*]; *"When you concentrate on a mental picture, it begins to stir, the image becomes enriched by details, it moves and develops. **Each time, naturally, you mistrust it and have the idea that you just made it up, that it is merely your own invention... It is not true...! We depend upon the benevolent*** *cooperation of our unconscious. If it does not cooperate we are completely lost ... Therefore I am convinced that we cannot do much in the way of conscious invention ... And so, when we concentrate on an inner picture and we are careful not to interrupt the natural flow of events, our unconscious will produce a series of images that will make up a complete story."*

Also, consider that another major reason why a rope might be a powerful representation of the qualities of our relationships is the fact that *for each of us, life literally began by being connected by a 'rope' to another person.*

Each human fetus spends months connected by an umbilical cord [i.e., a **rope**] to its mother. Some clinicians, perhaps especially those of a Freudian or Jungian persuasion, may choose to argue that our unconscious minds retain that earliest of our experiences and that ropes thereafter will hold for us the essence of fundamental connections to other persons.

As compelling as that notion may be, however, it is not necessary to believe that one of the reasons that the Rope Trick works so well is because of deep-seated memories of our umbilical cord attachments to our mothers, since the very nature of a rope, i.e., its characteristics and functions, primarily involves connecting one object [or person] to another. On the other hand, I think you may agree, that the initial connection between fetus and mother is an interesting and perhaps suggestive factoid.

Then, Dr Cupchik, let me rephrase my question: Might not a person *who is already familiar with* **the Rope Trick exercise, attempt to consciously force it into a particular kind of imagery sequence?**

Recall case # 2, that of Mary, the individual who described seeing herself and her husband in a desert-like landscape with a lone, leafless dead tree between them. She had imagined herself holding in her hands both ends of a thick rope, one end of which was in the form of a noose and in her imagery she saw herself looking about for a suitable branch of the tree from which to suspend the rope in order to hang her husband. She told me that this imagery had upset her very much; she was extremely uncomfortable with its very blatantly suggestive implications and said that, several times, she attempted to deliberately change it to a more pleasant image - but the 'noose' imagery kept reappearing in the sequence in her conscious mind. This may well be an example of the unconscious exerting a considerable influence over the conscious mind, even if the conscious level of the mind is distinctly unhappy with that of which it is becoming aware.

It must still be acknowledged, nevertheless, that perhaps it is *possible* to deliberately distort or modify the Rope Trick exercise in order to produce a more or less 'favourable' or 'desirable' experience than is probably the more accurate. However, decades of experience with hundreds of users of this mental imagery exercise have shown that most persons will simply 'go with the flow' and allow their subconscious and unconscious minds to provide them with imagery sequences that do indeed appear to have some validity. An exception here might be an instance where the person is simply *not at all ready* to see the truth about his or her relationship with another. However, one of the remarkable qualities of the Rope Trick exercise is that these persons will sometimes break through their own defensive postures and reveal that which is truer for them about the relationship.

Therefore it is important to realize that in carrying out the Rope Trick exercise, what you find may be not at all what you had expected, and if you are not ready to accept the mental imagery experience as possibly valid should it be uncomfortable to you, then you would be well advised to *not* carry out the exercise, or at least do so only if you are in treatment with a suitable psychotherapist.

The emotional learnings that the Rope Trick responses may also provide.
The learnings that may take place as individuals consider their imaginative imagery experiences, are not restricted to *intellectual* insight. *Emotional* gains may also take place. The imager's immediate

emotional state can influence image formation, and, in turn, can itself be influenced by his or her imagery experience. This latter factor, the alteration of one's emotional state by the imagery experience, means that emotional learning can take place.

Again recall Case # 1, that of Lynda, as a case in point. When she had her imagery of attempting to pull both herself and her husband up the knee-deep, snow-filled embankment, she described feeling an emotional release of what had been pent up anger and resentment, and soon after she had her Rope Trick experience she confronted her husband about his lack of contribution to the marriage.

****

CASE # 6: CLAIRE, THE SINGLE, 50 YEAR OLD CLIENT WHO NEVER HAD MORE THAN THREE DATES WITH THE SAME MAN... AND THE MISSING ROPE.
Claire was one of the 40 subjects who took part in my dissertation experiment, and she carried out the Rope Trick exercise with her most recent boyfriend in mind. Fifty years of age, she was particularly interesting from a psychological perspective because, although she was arguably above average in intelligence, education and appearance, she had not ever, in her life, had more than three dates with the same man. In my office I noted that she avoided eye contact and tended to be hardly audible. As I did with the other 39 subjects, and because the subjects' own words were so very important, all their Rope Trick responses were not only written longhand by themselves, but as well, they all offered a spoken version as well. In fact, both my verbal instructions to them in leading them through the Rope Trick [I actually read the exercise out loud to each person from a prepared script – a version of which was presented earlier in this book] as well as their responses to the exercise, were all recorded. What I instructed each of them to do, in part, was as follows: *"Keeping your eyes closed, please re-run the imagery experience that you have just had, from the beginning, and describe it out loud, in the present tense, as if it is happening now for the first time."*

The most remarkable aspect of Claire's rendition of her otherwise rather bland response was what she did <u>not</u> say; *she never mentioned a rope* while reciting her experience to me. When I then inquired about the rope she seemed genuinely confused and asked, "What rope are you referring to?" I reminded her that I had asked her, five different times in fact, to include some sort of rope in the imagery sequence, but she said that she did not hear that instruction and did not believe I had given it.

Now the fact was, as I just stated, that I read the entire instructions for the Rope Trick exercise from a printed text and it specifically mentioned the rope on those five occasions. Nevertheless, Claire vehemently denied that I had ever made any mention of a rope when I gave her the instructions for the imagery exercise. Thankfully, because I had recorded my verbal instructions to the 40 subjects, I replayed the recording of Claire's Rope Trick instructions and sure enough, there was my mentioning the rope again and again. Claire was astounded and once more reiterated that she had no recollection of me mentioning a rope.

Interestingly, Claire has been the only one of the many hundreds persons to whom I have personally administered the Rope Trick mental imagery exercise these past over four decades who did *not* include some sort of rope in her verbal rendering of her mental imagery experience. I suggest that the absence of a rope in her Rope Trick experience says a great deal about Claire's manner of relating to men. Which is to say, *she didn't! Hardly at all.*

Although Claire was a highly educated, presentable and intelligent woman, <u>she was likely largely intellectually and emotionally *absent* when in the company of men</u>, and that probably had to do with her ways of having dealt with the severe emotional and sexual abuse she had experienced as a child. Suffice to say that she simply didn't 'relate' to men, even when she was physically present. Therefore it is hardly surprising that she had not had more than three dates with any one man. The lack of a rope in her Rope Trick response suggests that her unconscious had likely recognised that the notion of a rope represented that of a relationship, and therefore, 'no relationship, no rope', was evident in Claire's Rope Trick experience.

****

Chapter 7

THE 'ROPE TRICK' EXERCISE MAY HAVE A THERAPEUTIC EFFECT

The therapeutic aspect of the Rope Trick mental imagery exercise

It is both accurate and important to note that, as was the cases of Lynda, Case # 1 and Wayne, Case # 5 in the last chapter, that the Rope Trick sometimes has a *therapeutic* effect in addition to its *assessment* function. On many occasions, as a result of having just done the Rope Trick exercise, clients have reported experiencing cognitive [i.e., thinking] and/or affective [i.e., emotional] *shifts* in their perceptions of the relationships they were examining.

In some instances the shifts have been positive; they now had more positive thoughts and/or warmer emotions towards the other person. In other cases, however, their views have moved in the negative direction, in the sense that their new thoughts and/or emotions regarding their relationships had prompted them to view them in a less favourable light and they were motivated to take new actions as a result.

****

Having carried on psychotherapy with couples for more than thirty-five years it is clear to me that some individuals arrive at their therapists' offices too late for relationship repair work to be effective. A crude analogy might be deciding to tow one's car in for a long-delayed oil change only after its motor has seized up.

CASE # 7: HANK AND NADINE, A YOUNG MARRIED COUPLE WHO CAME TO COUNSELING TOO LATE.

Some time ago a handsome and intelligent married couple arrived at my office, it turned out, at the insistence of the wife. She had pleaded with her husband to not initiate a marital separation immediately, but to give therapy a last 'Hail Mary' sort of chance.

It turned out that with this particular couple, the husband, Hank, had implored Nadine, his wife of seven years, to come for counseling numerous times in the past, as it became increasingly clear to him that he was more and more resentful of her oft-expressed disinterest in having almost anything to do with his interests, friends, siblings or other members of his extended family. Nadine appeared to only want to either have him to herself, or in the company of her own friends and family. Her inflexibility in this regard had become a very big turnoff for Hank, as he missed seeing his friends and family members... *a lot!*

Cut off from his close contacts and cultural interests by Nadine's pressuring him to do so, Hank had finally had enough, and told her that, given that he had consistently extended himself to accommodate to her interests and other relationships for years, that it was now crucially important to him that she attempt to reciprocate. She time and again refused to do so. However, when Hank told Nadine that he had finally reached the point of no return and that he intended to separate, Nadine relented and said that she really did want the marriage to work and that she was willing to try and change. She pleaded with Hank to go with her for couples counseling.

After two sessions of introductory couples counseling, Hank told his wife while he was in my office that he realized that he had fallen out of love with her some time earlier. **His Rope Trick mental imagery response seemed to corroborate his statement.** His response was one in which he saw that he had let go of the rope and walked away after imagining himself having become exhausted in an seemingly endless tug of war with his wife. As he imagined himself leaving the scene he said that his primary emotions were of deep sadness but also of great relief.

Unfortunately it does happen that some couples make an attempt at counseling when it really is possibly too late to recover. In spite of her highly emotional pleadings, Hank did separate from Nadine a few weeks after our last joint session.

****

CASE # 8: SAM & VERONICA: 28 YEARS AND A DETERIORATING MARRIAGE WAS TOO MUCH.

Sam and Veronica arrived at my office about four years after their youngest child had finished university and moved out of town for a good job and they had finally been left entirely on their own. A wealthy couple who had been able to take advantage of many of the best and most varied vacations and other experiences together and with their family over the previous 28 years, Veronica described Sam as a very bitter, angry and demeaning person who tended to take out his frustrations on her via verbally sarcastic and abusive comments at any time of day or night. When she let him know in a most definitive fashion that she had had enough and wanted out of the marriage, Sam asked his wife to attempt counseling as a last ditch effort to save their relationship.

Interestingly, but not surprisingly, these two individuals' Rope Trick responses were very different from one another.

Veronica's exercise produced an imagery sequence in which her husband was using the rope in a very aggressive manner, shaking it violently back and forth while both held on, until she imagined that she let go of her end of the rope in order to ease the physical pain she was imagining experiencing.

Sam's Rope Trick experience was markedly different. He saw his wife as attempting to tie him up and he was trying to break loose from an ever-tightening rope. He clearly saw himself as acting out in order to escape her grip.

I had seen Sam first for a session, followed by his wife for her session, and then the two of them together – this format is one I use very frequently in order to meet each member of a couple one-on-one so as to establish a relationship with each of them as individuals and to allow each client to discuss concerns without needing to couch words so as not to upset a possibly defensive or vulnerable partner.

Towards the end of the first joint session Veronica and Sam announced that they were going to the Caribbean for a week and would be staying at a high-end resort for what they both described as a last-ditch attempt to rekindle their close feelings for one another. When they next arrived at my office after they had returned from their holiday Sam sat very quiet while Veronica expressed the fact that she had decided before they went south that she was going to do everything possible to please Sam in order to ensure that he would have nothing to become distressed about during the holiday.

She described how, day after day, the weather and the facilities of the resort were outstanding; their meals were wonderful, and their sexual relations had evidently been highly satisfying to Sam and pleasing to her, as well. However, as their holiday was drawing to a close she recounted that one day when they were at the beach, relaxing and reading on their chaise lounges, and Veronica had nearly convinced herself that her husband was perhaps finally changing, suddenly Sam threw down the book he was reading onto the sand and began to berate his wife over something that had happened many months before. After being subjected to his yelling, swearing and insulting her for nearly a full half-hour, Veronica recalled for me that she had had a very powerful visualization.

She reported that she had spontaneously imagined that a huge master switch located in the middle of her chest aggressively moved from the 'on' to the 'off' position. She described that this 'switching off' had been accompanied by an almost overwhelming sensation of her affection for Sam evaporating. The new state of her feelings had not left her from that moment to the time that they reappeared in my office. Veronica simply said, in a level, unemotional tone, "I'm done." And evidently, she was.

The Rope Trick mental imagery exercise may produce positive or negative experiences.

While it is true that the Rope Trick exercise may produce *positive changes* in an individual's thoughts and/or feelings in regard to a particular relationship, the opposite may also occur. It does happen that the user of the exercise might have a realization that may prompt him or her to alter how to function in a relationship in the future. So, clearly there is no guarantee that the use of the Rope Trick - or any other psychological tool or technique for that matter - will necessarily improve a relationship. However, most people would probably agree that it is best to have as much information as possible when attempting to understand and deal with an upsetting situation, particularly when it involves a business or a personal relationship.

Aspects of the rope may change during the Rope Trick exercise.

On many occasions users of the Rope Trick have reported experiencing *changes* in their thoughts about, and feelings towards, the other persons during the imagery sequences, and these changes are sometimes reflected in changes in the characteristics and/or functions of the rope seen in the imagery sequence from the first time it is viewed to when it is described again later on.

For instance, one user, a once highly paid graphics designer who had decided to retire, initially described the rope as being in very poor condition, with one end tied around her ankle while the other end was being held by her husband and she was just tagging along behind him. However, as the imagery sequence progressed, *the rope appeared to change* into one that was in much better condition and was now being held in the hands of both persons who were now moving along side by side.

Later, when we reviewed the imagery she had described, she stated that she was only partially aware of the fact that the condition and position of the rope *had changed during the course of her imagery experience*. However, she also said that she was now feeling better about the relationship with her husband than she had been before carrying out the exercise, and was determined to stop perceiving herself as a victim in relation to him; she said that she had just decided, even while sitting in my office doing the exercise, to go back to work at least part-time so that she would stop feeling so dependent upon him for financial support and also so that she would feel better about herself. This shift in feelings about herself and what new actions she intended to take in her life emerged even as she had gone through, and afterwards discussed, her Rope Trick experience.

A Caution: occasionally the shift in thoughts and/or feelings towards the other person may release very strong, pent up positive -or negative- emotions.

As was described in the first case discussed in this book, when Lynda [Case # 1] saw herself dragging her passive husband up a knee-deep, snow covered hill, she expressed very strong negative feelings about her husband's lack of contribution to their joint task, i.e., getting out of debt and getting on with their lives. It was very important to provide this client with an opportunity to discuss, in the safety of the therapy session, the fact that she was now feeling very angry indeed towards her husband. As experienced psychotherapists will be aware, it is important, to the extent that it is appropriate, to provide clients with the opportunity to express their feelings in a safe situation.

It is also important to remind clients that even if their imagery sequences involved some sort of violence, this does not mean that they actually want to - or should, of course - act out violently towards other persons in their waking lives. Dreaming of causing violence during a night dream, similarly, does not mean or suggest that the dreamer should act on that imagery. Rather, it is important to be willing to receive the messages of the Rope Trick [or the night dream] as suggestive, not as directives, and they may assist us to recognize feelings that may have greater symbolic than literal value.

Also, as Freud himself might have said, *"Sometimes a cigar is just a cigar [i.e., not a phallic symbol]"* and therefore all imagery content should be considered to be suggestive only and not necessarily intended to be taken literally.

Chapter 8

DIFFERING INTERPRETATIONS OF A PARTICULAR 'ROPE TRICK' RESPONSE

Often there is more than one way to interpret an individual's Rope Trick response – and differing interpretations may all have at least some validity. Carrying out the Rope Trick exercise is rather like having a so-called directed daydream – or a night dream, for that matter. Like all day -or night- dreams, nearly all are open to differing interpretations. Of course, it may also be conceivable that the content of a day or night dream [or a Rope Trick response] is essentially meaningless, *but possibly not too often!*

The reader can find many books dealing with the interpretation of dreams. The fact that there are sometimes differing –or even opposing-interpretations of the same imagery symbol or sequence should not deter you from considering the potential value of exploring their *varied* possible meanings. In fact, even seemingly opposing interpretations may both have some validity.

[I happen to have a colleague and close friend who, like myself, was first a professional engineer but also has a Ph.D. in psychology. We are actually adherents of different 'schools' of psychology, yet we do, in fact, occasionally discuss our dreams with one another and share our interpretations. Even though we frequently come up with very different interpretations [he is a 'Jungian' while I am more of a Freudian and Gestalt-oriented dream interpreter], usually both our two however differing interpretations have at least some validity. The varying interpretations may be like different views of a three-dimensional puzzle, each having some validity when viewed from our differing locations.]

Using a mental imagery exercise such as the Rope Trick can facilitate different levels of your mind to communicate with each other.

Using the Rope Trick 'invites' the unconscious and/or subconscious to communicate with the conscious mind, via visual images. Likewise, when a poet, novelist, sculptor, architect, scientist or artist [or the creator of virtually any innovative project, for that matter] is engaged in the imaginative process, that person's various levels of mind are likely communicating with one another.

The unconscious mind readily recognizes what the concept of a rope symbolizes.

Our unconscious minds appear to readily recognize the symbolic meanings of objects without having been formally educated or consciously instructed to do so. As an analogy, the observer of a painting, a movie, a car, a house or another object, may find it appealing or appalling at a conscious level without necessarily recognizing why. That person's unconscious mind may be responding to the content of the painting [movie, car, or whatever] according to his own prior experiences, interpretations and memories. The expression, "different strokes for different folks" refers to the fact that different people may respond very differently to the same stimulus [a painting, book, movie, car, etc...] based upon their own personalities, interests, personal histories and the associations they may make to the same content – without necessarily ever consciously recognizing why. The expression, "I like [don't like] 'it'; I am not sure why," is a response that most of us have had at one time or another to a particular play, piece of music, car, etc...

It is well known, of course, that different people may ascribe different meanings to the same object. Some vigorously investigated psychological tools such as the famous Rorschach inkblots have actually been found to be perceived and responded to in somewhat similar ways by persons who have certain psychological qualities or characteristics in common, while individuals who have very different psychological make-ups may respond to the same Rorschach cards remarkably differently. Consequently it is possible, by giving an individual the Rorschach, to make some generalizations about that person's mind [or psyche]. Of course, no psychological tool or test is infallible, but administered by a clinician who is highly experienced and expert in the administration and interpretation of such a psychological device, it is usually possible to provide some valuable information about the psyche of an individual. As an example, sexually immature adults often produce very different interpretations of certain of the Rorschach cards than other adults whose sexual development is more age appropriate.

In the case of the Rope Trick, decades of administering this particular mental imagery exercise have clearly indicated that the unconscious minds of most individuals, no matter what their intellectual ability or how sophisticated [or naïve] they may be in terms of psychological awareness, are entirely capable of recognizing the possible symbolic meanings of the ropes in their imagery sequences, and that they might have relevance to their actual relationships at the times that they do the exercise.

Chapter 9

EVERY OBJECT OR ACTION HAS A SYMBOLIC AS WELL AS A LITERAL MEANING

Every object or action usually has two meanings – a literal and a symbolic one.
This is a very important concept to keep in mind, whether doing the Rope Trick or carrying out any other act, such as, for example, shopping for an item of clothing, a car or home, or engaging in an interaction with someone.

For example, consider that at a specific moment in time, a particular brand and model of car may be considered 'in' or 'cool' or 'with it' or special in some other way. The vehicle one drives, the clothes one wears, the kind of watch one has on one's wrist (or not), the make of smartphone one may have, all may be considered to 'say something' about the owner or user; that is to say, they may have a symbolic meaning as well as a literal one.

Let's consider the automobile as an example. Virtually all cars serve the same essential function, namely getting a person from point X to point Y. But the symbolic meaning of driving a high-end, very expensive vehicle such as a Rolls Royce or a Porsche projects a different 'message' to observers than if one were driving a relatively inexpensive and more common vehicle such as a Honda Civic or Toyota Corolla. The 'message' that is sent may be that the person driving the far more expensive car is relatively wealthier, more powerful *[How many horsepower does your car's engine have?]* and/or possibly more important in some way than the person who arrives at the same destination in a Civic or Corolla.

Of course, on the other hand, a very wealthy and powerful individual may wish to project an image of being [or may actually be] modest and/or frugal and in might to choose to drive, say, a Toyota

63

Prius, as a conscious and/or unconscious expression of those personal traits or philosophies.

When one wishes to impress others, one might carefully choose [to the extent one can] what one wears, drives, etc... Of course, the fact is that the 'message' [i.e., symbolic meaning] one wishes to send, and that which is actually received, may be very different. One may wish to simply send a message of frugality by driving a Prius, while an observer may infer that the user of such a car might be a Democrat, a 'tree hugger', very wise, a miser and/or downright cheap. In each case, the symbolic meaning that one observer attributes to the use of a particular kind of vehicle [or any other item] may be quite different than that which may be intended to be conveyed by the user.

By extension of the above reasoning, it is important to consider that whatever characteristics and functions of the rope and the particular actions of the persons observed within a Rope Trick experience, one should probably interpret the imagery response with caution.

At the same time, while keeping this caveat in mind, the characteristics and functions of the rope and the actions of the individuals in the Rope Trick imagery sequence often *do* have relevant symbolic meanings. Practice in using and interpreting Rope Trick responses will often allow the user to arrive at a pertinent understanding of what the various facets of the Rope Trick response might mean, and to do so more and more quickly over time.

****

The literal and symbolic meanings of the rings people wear.
A piece of string or metal or any other material wrapped around one's finger often has a symbolic significance to the wearer. Consider a ring made of gold or silver, perhaps with one or more diamonds embedded in it, worn on a finger of the left hand; such a ring might be meant to signify that one is engaged or married.

As it happens, I wear a wedding ring made of the precious metals of *gold* and *platinum* and valued at over $1000. I also wear a very plain ring on my little finger made of *stainless steel* that costs substantially less – actually about $30, or less than $1/30^{th}$ of the value of my wedding ring. While the stainless steel or so-called 'iron' ring is literally merely just a piece of very inexpensive metal, hardly a month goes by when someone in my home country of Canada doesn't happen to notice that ring and say something like, "Ah, I see you are a professional engineer; what kind of engineer are you?" As it happens, in Canada university engineering graduates, shortly after successfully completing their academic studies and certain other requirements, take part in an 'iron ring' ceremony and we wear our iron rings proudly.

[Incidentally, about fifteen years ago I gave a talk on a psychological topic to a women's club in Toronto at which time I was introduced as a psychologist who had been an electrical engineering graduate of McGill University. At the end of the talk a member of the audience approached asked if I had taken part in the 'iron ring' ceremony after graduation. When I replied in the affirmative she asked why I was not then wearing my iron ring. I replied that I had actually lost it during a move some 20-plus years earlier and since I was no longer working as an engineer I did not want to misrepresent myself by getting another one. She then introduced herself as the former Dean of engineering at a major Canadian university and told me that, since I had taken part in the 'iron ring' ceremony, I was fully entitled to continue to wear the ring. Soon afterwards I applied to the appropriate university office and acquired a new one, which I have been proudly wearing ever since.]

My modest iron ring reminds me of my first [and by far my most challenging] university Bachelors program and of my time working as an engineer decades ago, designing navigational guidance systems for the then-next generation of military aircraft. My wedding ring and iron ring 'mean' a great deal to me [i.e., symbolically, of course] and I wear them both with pride and pleasure having nothing whatsoever to do with their markedly different metallic makeups and monetary values.

The titles that just precede our names may have both literal and symbolic meanings:
Our titles [Ms, Mrs, Mr, Dr, Father, Imam or Rabbi, M'am, Sir, Gramps, etc...] are meant to convey something about us, our so-called 'status' or jobs or ages, and possibly even our self-perceptions or identities. For many of us, the change in our status when a title is still relatively new is something that can take getting used to. Medical students are often called "Dr." even before they graduate; this helps prepare them to accept their new position in society while at the same time getting at least some of their patients to view them as perhaps more deserving than they yet are of that title. In any case, the bestowing of a 'moniker' such as Dr., Father, etc..., often does have an effect on both the recipient who is being addressed in this way and on the person who uses such a title when addressing someone.

Virtually every action we take – or choose to *not* take – may also have a symbolic as well as a literal meaning.
How we greet another person can also convey something of symbolic value. For example, an expert in preparing individuals for job interviews recently informed me that research has shown that there is one particular action that, should the person *not* carry it out, virtually guarantees that he will *not* get the job.

What is this action? It is the very simple act of *smiling*. Evidently, if the job applicant does not smile when first meeting the person doing the hiring, that lack of a positive non-verbal action is often *interpreted* by the prospective employer as signalling [rightly or wrongly] that the applicant may not be as likely to get along with other workers as another applicant who smiles easily at first contact. The smile not only usually looks pleasant but also *symbolizes* warmth and approachability.

Shaking hands – a nearly universal multi-meaning symbol
Consider next the common act of shaking hands with someone. Literally, of course, shaking hands involves extending a hand to reach out and shake that of another person. But symbolically a handshake is also usually meant to convey a friendly, non-threatening greeting, suggested perhaps by the fact that the hand being offered is [presumably] not bearing a weapon at the same time.

As the reader likely knows, both hand shakers may also be aware of [and may even be scrutinizing] the physical qualities of the hand being shaken;

- Is the other person's handshake strong or weak *[and what might one presume from this in regard to the other person's assertiveness, strength of character, aggressiveness?]*;

- Is the hand being offered dry or clammy *[i.e., is the other person relaxed or anxious?]*;

- Is the handshake short or long in duration *[and might a very short handshake indicate a desire to minimize any suggestion of intimacy? On the other hand, does a handshake of very long duration suggest an attempt at taking control or forcing intimacy?]*, and...

- Does the other person shake your hand vigorously, just right or does his hand hardly move at all? *[A very vigorous handshake may seem overly enthusiastic, or if the other person's hand hardly moves, does that suggest a weak interest in any involvement?]*

I still recall being quite shocked when, many years ago, what I presumed would just be a 'normal' shaking of the hand of a locally prominent elected official, ended up with him firmly grasping and holding onto my hand for nearly a full two minutes while pulling me towards him so that I was being moved off balance. Was the politician being overly intimate, merely very *[too very]* friendly, outright controlling or some combination of these and/or other possibilities? Many of us may 'read' into such things as a seemingly overly assertive or aggressive handshake or one where the other person pulls us very close and then does not let go of our hand for an extended period of time.

*[Interestingly, I happened to recently view on television a famous movie, **The Maltese Falcon**, starring Humphrey Bogart. At one point in the film, Bogart shakes hand with a very large, powerful and sinister individual played by Sydney Greenstreet. The latter actually kept holding Bogart's hand and arm as he leads him about a dozen feet, around some furniture and to a chair where he wished to seat him – clearly a very controlling, and perhaps an even threatening gesture.]*

Whether one is offering a glass of water to an elderly grandparent, smiling at a young child, or offering a gift to a friend – all these and most other actions may have a symbolic meaning as well as a literal one.

****

CASE # 9: TOM AND THE POSSIBLE SYMBOLIC MEANING OF THE SEEMINGLY UNREASONABLE DEMAND OF HIS NOW-ADULT CHILD, FRANK, WHO AT THE TIME WAS MARRIED WITH CHILDREN OF HIS OWN.

Several years ago one of my clients, a retired gentleman in his late eighties [Tom], arrived for his session sporting a very perplexed facial expression. Evidently his 55 year old son, Frank, who lived across the continent in California, had recently taken my client to task, virtually demanding that he and his current wife purchase a condominium in Los Angeles close to where his son and family lived, and that they spend at least three months a year in L.A..

Tom was at a loss to understand why his son had become so upset when he said that spending so much time in L.A. was out of the question, given how physically and emotionally disruptive and exhausting it would be, and how to do so would severely strain the couple's retirement savings. As well, Tom elaborated, he already visited his son and family at least once a year for several days at a time, just as he did his other two grown children, all of whom were scattered about the USA.

As we discussed the matter further I learned that Frank was the youngest of his three children, and Tom admitted that he hadn't spent as much time with Frank when he was a youngster as he had with his two other siblings when they were children, since his at-that-time increased work responsibilities took him away from home for a substantial portion of the year, mostly during Frank's formative years. Now it seemed as if Frank was being quite unreasonable in demanding so much more time at this point in their lives.

I pointed out to Tom that it was distinctly possible that his youngest child's insistence that he spend more time close to him was likely even more important to Frank at a *symbolic* level rather than a literal one. Frank, I suggested, might still have some 'unfinished business' from his childhood, a time when he was dealing with a largely absent father. Tom said that throughout Frank's life, the latter had often expressed his resentment of his father's absences during his childhood, and Tom agreed that perhaps now Frank wanted to be somehow compensated for what he felt he had missed out on. Taking into account the fact that Tom and Frank spoke by telephone every couple of days and in recent years had also Skyped on a weekly basis, it was clear that Frank and Tom kept up a regular and substantial amount of communication. I suggested that Tom might consider discussing the possible symbolic component related to Frank's demand that Tom and his wife move out west, and perhaps agree to accompany his son to one or more of Frank's weekly counseling sessions with the psychologist he had been seeing for the previous two years. Tom readily agreed to offer to do so, as a means of hopefully assisting his son to achieve some 'closure' in this matter.

The Rope Trick mental imagery exercise is not a 'game'.

It is worthwhile reiterating that the Rope Trick is actually a powerful mental imagery exercise and it should not at all be considered some sort of 'parlour game'. At the same time, the Rope Trick can be used by most laypersons as often as desired, and each time it may well provide some insights into the status and dynamics of one of their relationships, if only the time is taken to consider the imagery response's symbolic meaning. Since the Rope Trick is a sort of 'dynamic thermometer' of an interpersonal relationship, it will likely help the person who uses it to better understand what is going on at that time in the relationship under consideration.

Chapter 10

THE 'BRIDGE TRICK' MENTAL IMAGERY EXERCISE

For the sake of carrying out an experimental investigation of *whether*, and if so, *why* the Rope Trick mental imagery exercise actually worked, I was called upon by my Ph.D. advisors to find some *thing* else that might work as well as a rope and explain in a rigorous manner how the alternative object was identified and why it would also be effective.
Describing the nearly five years of investigation that I carried out into why the Rope Trick worked and whether and why another object might also be effective in eliciting from the unconscious useful and understandable information regarding the status and dynamics of a relationship, is simply far beyond the scope or intention of this book. Anyone who is interested in reading about this should access my dissertation entitled 'Clinical Imaginative Imagery', my 1979 thesis submitted in conformity with the requirements for the Ph.D. degree at the University of Toronto.

Well, you might ask, *did* any other so-called 'seed image' other than a rope work as well in providing useful information about a relationship?
In order to answer that question I spent a considerable amount of time searching for another object that would work as well as a rope. In the course of my investigations I discarded many items, including such things as a rock, pencil, etc... Imagining a person, someone else and a *rock* [or *pencil*] in the same imagery sequence did not appear to offer nearly the flexibility and variety of possible events or circumstances as did a rope. But indeed, months of clinical investigation showed that *every* word or phrase that can be used to describe the *characteristics* and *functions* of a **bridge** can also be used to describe the characteristics and functions of a rope – or a relationship for that matter. Bridges, just like ropes and relationships, can be <u>strong</u> or <u>weak</u>, <u>thick</u> or <u>thin</u>, <u>new</u> or <u>old</u>, <u>flexible</u> or <u>rigid</u>, <u>long</u> or <u>short</u>, etc…

and that just as ropes may connect or otherwise involve two people or things, likewise so can bridges.

In fact, in my dissertation I offered the 'Bridge Trick' to nearly as many people as I did the Rope Trick and found that both versions had similar potency, i.e., the capacity to produce reliable and valid responses. The word "bridge" was merely substituted for the word "rope" in the verbatim rendition of the mental imagery exercise that I read aloud to almost half of the 40 subjects who took part in the experimental part of my dissertation. And indeed, the Bridge Trick worked virtually just as well as did the Rope Trick in revealing the status and dynamics of the subjects' interpersonal relationships.

My personal preference, however, remains the version that I initially developed, i.e., the *Rope Trick*, partly I am certain, because it was my original, intuitive creation; however, for variety, by all means feel free to use the word 'bridge' instead of the word 'rope' wherever it appears in the verbatim presentation.

****

CASE # 10: HARRIET, WHOSE 'BRIDGE TRICK" EXERCISE WAS RIGHT ON!
As was the case for all other 39 'subjects' who took part in my dissertation experiment, Harriett had agreed to come to my office to take part in "a mental imagery exercise".

[Incidentally, none of the subjects knew in advance that we would be focusing upon interpersonal relationships; all were simply told that we were interested in examining 'mental imagery', albeit at the Ph.D. level. Of course, all had the choice of stopping the imagery instructions at any time.]

Harriet went along with the entire Bridge Trick experience and when she was finished her verbal retelling was very vivid indeed. She said, *"I and my husband of 25 years are on opposite sides of a very old, very dilapidated, shit-covered bridge that is falling down. It really looks disgusting and I am walking away in a direction opposite from him.* "

When we were discussing what meaning the Bridge Trick experience had for her, she replied just as forcibly, saying, *"Well, I didn't want to break my appointment with you since I knew this was for your Ph.D. study. But the fact is that I am flying out to Seattle later today and will be staying out there. I am separating from my husband for good! Our marriage is just like that bridge that I saw: very old, covered in shit, and broken down."*

A Caveat worth repeating: The Rope Trick and Bridge Trick are not intellectual 'games', and care must be taken when employing them; What follows is an actual example of when using these mental imagery exercises, it turned out, was *not* appropriate. In the 1980s a psychologist who was also on staff at the Clarke Institute of Psychiatry where I was working at the time and who knew about the Rope Trick mental imagery exercise and its evident potency, asked me whether I might give it to prison inmates who were part of a research study of violent rapists/murderers that was being conducted at the time. I agreed, but after one of these convicted rapist/murderers had finished the relaxation phase of the Rope Trick exercise and I then asked him to imagine himself, <u>another person</u> and a rope in the same scene, he opened his eyes, sat straight up and said, *"I don't want to do this! I have been getting training in 'thought-stopping' and as soon as you gave me the instructions for the exercise, I saw myself and a young woman in the same scene, and I am not supposed to allow myself to imagine any scene that has a woman in it!"*

Of course, I immediately accepted this man's decision to decline to carry out the exercise. Incidentally, this was the only occasion over these past more than 40 years that someone has declined to carry out the Rope Trick or Bridge Trick exercises. Usually people are very curious and look forward to learning another way of considering their relationships.

Chapter 11

THE EXCEPTIONAL SYMBOLIC POTENCY
OF A ROPE-BRIDGE

Since ropes and bridges have each been shown to symbolize the status and dynamics of relationships, what about the possible symbolic potency of their combination, namely 'rope-bridges'?
In the years since I created the Rope Trick and then later found that the Bridge Trick was also effective in symbolizing the status and dynamics of a relationship, I have often thought about the 'draw' that rope-bridges have for many of us. Of course, there are an innumerable number of 'rope-bridges' in existence, including in more primitive countries where vines and branches are among the chief building materials used in such structures. Even so-called first-world countries sometimes use bridges that utilize ropes [though frequently in the form of steel cables; they are often referred to as 'wire ropes'] that are strung across rivers or canyons.

For example, less than 4 miles from North Vancouver, British Columbia, is the Capilano Suspension Bridge, located within Capilano Provincial Park. That bridge, consisting mostly of steel cables and a wooden floor, extends some 450 feet across and 230 feet above the Capilano river. It is worthwhile pointing out that this suspension bridge is a tourist attraction all on its own; going across it and walking back is rather like going on a ride at an amusement park; it doesn't really lead anywhere special. One goes across it simply for the experience of having done so.

The bridge's website [www.capbridge.com] proudly states that since it was originally constructed in 1889, *millions* of people have chosen to walk across the bridge and back, the vast majority evidently for the sheer pleasure and thrill of so doing. Surely that is rather representative of the psychological 'pull' of rope-bridges; if the bridge were constructed of metal trusses only, rigidly welded together to form a means of crossing the Capilano Canyon, I suspect that a substantially smaller number of persons might be attracted to go out of their way in order to cross it.

Now, of course, the Capilano Suspension Bridge has an actual 'give' to it, and people crossing it likely experience excitement due to the fact that they can feel the rope-bridge move beneath their feet as they walk across it.

[Even some bridges made of steel trusses may have some 'give' to them, although that is not usually a welcome or intended feature; I well remember the hundreds of crossings that my father and I made in his car during my childhood, of the Victoria Bridge that connects the island of Montreal with the city of Saint-Lambert on the south shore. Trust me; crossing that vibrating steel truss bridge did not have quite the same cache as traversing the Capilano span, although given its age even at that time [having been originally built in 1859] and the fact that cars tended to slither somewhat sideways even as they made their way along the bridge *was* rather stirring – if not nerve-racking. However, I doubt that many people relished that experience or chose to deliberately go out of their way to cross it for its own sake.]

Other examples of suspension *rope-bridges* include the Golden Gate Bridge in California, the Lions Gate Bridge in Vancouver, Canada and the Clifton Suspension Bridge in the UK. All of them have been magnets not only for those who enjoy the thrill of walking across them but also, unfortunately, for many others bent upon suicide.

Interestingly, there have even been reports of individuals crossing the Oakland-Bay Bridge [a steel truss bridge that joins the city of Oakland to San Francisco] in order to get to the Golden Gate Bridge, some 10 miles and more than a half-hour away, to carry out their intended acts of self-destruction. It seems clear that, given the choice, more people prefer to jump off a rope-bridge [i.e., a so-called suspension bridge] than a truss-type structure.

Why might this be the case? As was amply demonstrated in my graduate work and throughout this book, there is a very distinct likelihood that our unconscious minds recognize that ropes and bridges symbolically represent the status and dynamics of interpersonal relationships. I suggest that for persons who intend <u>to permanently cut off all relationships with other persons and this world</u>, the 'psychological pull' to do so by jumping off of a 'rope-bridge', for example the Golden Gate Bridge, might perhaps be the ultimate act.

Readers interested in learning somewhat more about the apparent pull of rope-bridges in general and the Golden Gate bridge in particular, including for those intent upon ending *all* their relationships, will find additional information in Appendix A near the end of this book.

IN CONCLUSION

I sincerely hope that you have enjoyed reading this book and that you have gained insights from using the Rope Trick mental imagery exercise yourself, and if you are a counsellor or psychotherapist, by using it with your clients, as well. At the least I expect that you may have become more sensitized to the fact that <u>most objects and actions have *symbolic* as well as *literal* aspects</u> to them. I can attest to the fact that accepting this truth over the past decades has helped me to appreciate the possible multiple meanings of actions and objects.

Marshall McLuhan, a renowned former professor at University of Toronto who wrote the best seller, *The Medium Is The Message,* was undoubtedly correct when he stated that, "A message isn't a message until it gets read." I would only add that, because it is possible to attribute more than one meaning to many – and possibly even most – messages, it is vitally important to be careful when attempting to send a message so that, hopefully, it will not be *mis*read. It often helps to follow up a written message with a phone call as well to make it more likely that the message that one intended to convey was, in fact, that which was received. Nowadays, emails are recognized as notorious for too often being misread or misunderstood.

Should you choose to share your Rope Trick experiences and the relevance that you attribute to them, by all means feel free to write to me at *wcupchik@aol.com*. You will understand that I may not offer a reply but if possible, I certainly will read all your renditions. Meanwhile, I sincerely hope that you will find, as have so many others, that the Rope Trick mental imagery exercise will serve you very well indeed.

APPENDICES

Five appendices appear in the following pages. They are offered as a means of providing some additional information for interested readers.

Appendix A is titled **SAN FRANCISCO'S GOLDEN GATE BRIDGE – A PARTICULARLY POWERFUL LURE FOR PERSONS BENT ON COMMITTING SUICIDE.** I have included it because it demonstrates, I believe, the exceptional potency of 'rope-bridges' when it comes to speaking to our unconscious minds about the symbolism of ropes, bridges and relationships.

Appendix B, titled **THE THREE TYPES OF SYMBOLIC ENCODING,** is included for the interest of those readers who may be interested in an elaboration of what different *kinds* of symbolic encoding exist.

Appendix C, titled **THE TWO MAIN KINDS OF CLINICAL IMAGERY,** is intended to differentiate the different kinds of mental imagery exercises that are employed by psychotherapists.

Appendix D, titled **TWO PEOPLE DON'T HAVE A RELATIONSHIP: THEY HAVE AT LEAST TWO!** is provided for readers who may wish to know more about what that statement actually means and to assist them to appreciate why it is that it is so important for the two members of a couple to recognize that fact.

Appendix E, titled **AN EXCEPTIONAL EXAMPLE OF THE SYMBOLIC MEANING OF A PHYSICAL OBJECT,** offers a powerful case in point.

APPENDIX A

SAN FRANCISCO'S GOLDEN GATE BRIDGE – A POWERFUL LURE FOR SO MANY PEOPLE, INCLUDING THOSE DETERMINED TO COMMIT SUICIDE

I first walked across the Golden Gate Bridge in 1972, on my first visit to California to attend a month-long training workshop for psychotherapists. Since then I have visited and walked back and forth across that magnificent structure on more than twenty occasions.

As a former professional engineer I have always been in awe of the incredible technical accomplishment that this bridge truly is. At 8,981 feet in length, with a span that measures 4200 feet in length, and with 220 feet vertical clearance at high tide, the bridge provides a marvellous entryway to the Pacific Ocean from the mouth of San Francisco Bay.

For the more technically minded, the following information was derived from Wikipedia in March 2015. "The weight of the roadway is hung from two cables that passed through the two main towers and are fixed in concrete at each end. Each cable is made of 27,572 strands of wire. There are 80,000 miles [130,000 km] of wire in the main cables. Each strand of wire is approximately 1/5 of an inch diameter." Ropes that are made from metal strands are often called 'wire ropes', and the Golden Gate Bridge is a marvellous example of such a structure.

As one for whom photography has been a hobby for over 60 years, attempting to capture some sense of the grandeur and wonder that is the Golden Gate Bridge has been a wonderful challenge these last many years. Happily, and although I have photographed the bridge a great many times during my various visits, I believe I can truly say that my October 2013 visit afforded me an incomparable opportunity to record some of the bridge's most awesome and visually thrilling moments, when an otherwise clear blue sky gifted the bridge with a lovely white, sharply delineated cloud and fog blanket that slipped just *under* its cables and *over* its roadway, and also extended wistfully over the Marin county hillside for several hundred feet.

Why the Golden Gate Bridge is such a 'magnet' for people to visit.

For reasons already provided at length in this book, *ropes* and *bridges* are exceptionally powerful symbolic tools with which to examine a relationship. I have also indicated, convincingly I believe, that our unconscious minds readily recognise this notion and that the Golden Gate Bridge, combining as it does both concepts within a scenic and architecturally magnificent 'rope-bridge', offers a virtually unparalleled opportunity for our unconscious minds to experience such a connection. As anyone who has walked across the Golden Gate will testify, the bridge literally moves and seems to be alive, in the sense that it vibrates, shakes and always seems to be changing in the vistas it offers, depending upon the fog or clouds or wind or rain or bright sunshine that can descend upon the bridge, and change rather suddenly sometimes, even during a single hour-long visit. Indeed, evidentially the Golden Gate Bridge was built to withstand up to 27 feet of lateral movement occasioned by very high winds. Having experienced many of these conditions during my various walks from the San Francisco side vista point to the Marin county side and back [or vice versa] I have always been in a state of sheer wonder and excitement of the experience, as I have never encountered the 'same' bridge twice.

Interestingly, on May 31st, 1987, the Golden Gate Bridge's 50th birthday, a birthday party of sorts was held for this magnificent structure. It was reported that more than 250,000 people chose to walk across the bridge on that occasion, resulting in an actual flattening of the arched deck, and causing the engineers responsible for the safety of the users and the bridge itself to close the entryway to more persons for fear that the load would become simply too much for the bridge to bear. I suggest that there are few other bridges that would have called forth such an outpouring of enthusiasm.

More on why the Golden Gate Bridge is also such a draw for persons contemplating suicide.
When deciding to cut off *all* relationships *permanently* by committing suicide, jumping off a bridge, preferably a rope-bridge, and in particular one that is universally recognized as being an optimal rope-bridge, may seem almost irresistible to the unconscious minds of many persons. So it is that the Golden Gate Bridge has been the stage for over 1200 suicide attempts, a number that has been exceeded only by persons who have leapt off the Nanjing Yangtze River Bridge in China [at about 2000 persons; source, Wikipedia, October 17, 2014]. However, given that since a Plexiglas barrier has been in place since 1993 to prevent suicides from the Chinese bridge and given that the population of Nanjing is about seven times that of San Francisco, the Golden Gate Bridge probably holds the unenviable record as the greatest 'magnet' for suicide-by-jumping-off-a-rope-bridge in the world. Apparently [and thankfully] in 2014, the authorities in charge of preventing such matters authorized spending funds to provide a suicide-prevention barrier across the length of the Golden Gate Bridge.

APPENDIX B

THE THREE TYPES OF SYMBOLIC ENCODING

Whether in works of art, design, night dreams or daytime imagery exercises such as the Rope Trick and Bridge Trick, there are essentially only three types of what are referred to as *symbolic encoding* **that can occur;** **condensation,** **displacement** *and* **symbolization.**

I - Condensation is a process resulting in the fusion of 2 or more images or ideas.

For example, such is the current connotation of the word "plastic" that imaging being handed a bouquet of flowers only to realize that they are made of plastic suggests not only that they are not living plants and are a poor substitute for the real thing, but perhaps the gesture of giving plastic flowers was itself 'plastic' or phony, and that the giver might not hold the recipient in high regard.

To take another example of condensation from the Rope Trick responses people have shared with me, consider that when the imager sees the other end of the rope tied around the other person at the level of the belly button, that may suggest that the other person is perceived as behaving in a rather immature or childish fashion in relation to the imager.

II - Displacement is the shift of emphasis or interest from one idea or image to another [usually less important in terms of relevance to conflictual or instinctual aims].

Dreams of having homosexual experiences with strangers may be somewhat less suggestive or threatening compared to dreams of heterosexual liaisons if the dreamer tends to hold orthodox views and is a deeply religious, heterosexual married man who is unwilling to acknowledge to himself that he is unhappy with his marital sex life. Of course, it is also possible that a married man unwilling to acknowledge and accept his sexual interest in males may imagine having extramarital encounters with females – or males.

III - <u>Symbolization</u> is the replacement of one idea or image by a visual presentation that may have various formal features in common with what is being symbolized but which disguises the latter's dynamic significance.

Thus, a man who is going into the hospital for a vasectomy may dream of the Tower of Pisa collapsing. Extensive analysis would probably be unnecessary to suggest the essence of his dream's symbolization.

****

Symbolic encoding may occur through the use of one or more of the three processes described above. In this book the general terms "symbolic encoding" and "symbolism" have both been used when referring to any such occurrences.

APPENDIX C

THE TWO MAIN KINDS OF <u>CLINICAL</u> IMAGERY

There are essentially at least two kinds of clinical imagery:
First is what may be called <u>clinical **instructed** imagery</u>, by which one means that the images that the individual is viewing are at all times in accordance with the therapist's instructions. Such *instructed imagery* sequences may be used in behavior modification, systematic desensitization, biofeedback, and a variety of meditations.

The other kind of clinical imagery I have termed <u>clinical **imaginative** imagery</u>. In 'clinical imaginative imagery' the images may begin with a therapist's suggestion of a so-called 'seed image' [e.g., a rope, bridge, house, etc...] but thereafter the imagery sequence is the unique production of the client's mental processes. Clinical imaginative imagery may be used in 'directed daydream' techniques, 'guided affective imagery', symbolic visualizations and other fantasy exercises.

APPENDIX D

MORE ABOUT WHY TWO PEOPLE DON'T HAVE 'ONE' RELATIONSHIP; THEY HAVE AT LEAST TWO RELATIONSHIPS

A vitally important point: two people do not have *a* relationship. Rather, there are always at least two relationships involved, specifically Person A's relationship with person B [about which A may, or may not, be satisfied] *and* person B's relationship with person A [about which B may, or may not, be content].

Not infrequently, A's relationship with B may not be very satisfying while B's relationship with A might be quite pleasing to B - or vice versa.

In order to evaluate the reliability and validity of the Rope Trick and Bridge Trick for my dissertation I developed what I termed the *Cupchik Relationship Questionnaire*, a 24-item, multiple choice questionnaire that assesses the adequacy of a relationship along four mutually independent factors: I labelled these factors [stated in *positive* terms]:

- Emotional Depth

- Mutual Dependency

- Balance Of Control
- *and*
- [Lack Of] Malice.

Over the last more than four decades I have asked couples from more than 20 cultures and languages whether, in their language and/or culture, they recognize that when they are referring to 'their relationship', that they are actually speaking of two different relationships. None of my clients have ever indicated that in their language or culture, such a distinction is made. I believe that this phenomenon is an example of what the renowned psychotherapist, Erich Fromm, referred to as a 'culturally patterned defect'; since essentially everyone in the same culture suffers from the same delusion or error and therefore no one recognizes that discussions of <u>our</u> relationship' are often bound to be, at the least, very frustrating, and may outright fail to accomplish very much - unless one of the parties is sufficiently persuasive and/or the other party 'gives up' or drops his or her defences.

Let me again emphasize this point: discussions about "<u>our</u> relationship" are often very frustrating and limited since there is really no such thing.

Discussions about 'our relationship' are almost bound to result in frustration and a failure to resolve major issues since the two parties are actually dealing with *two* different relationships. At the very least, it is important for the person who has the greatest concerns to say something akin to, "I am not comfortable [happy, satisfied, etc....,] *in my relationship* with you. I recognize that you may think things are going very well, perhaps because you are getting most of your needs and wants met from <u>your relationship</u> with me. But that is not true for me."

A vivid example of the fact that two people actually have two relationships with one another.

I well recall, even though it is more than 30 years ago, having a woman in her 50s in a therapy group I was leading who was particularly dejected, depressed and exhausted in large part as a result of her distinctly unsatisfactory marriage to a high-powered, evidently chauvinistic individual who rarely contributed time or effort to their family's goings-on.

On one occasion I saw this woman's husband when he arrived to pick her up; he virtually glowed in his full-length cashmere coat, appearing to be very healthy and robust and in such contrast to the bedraggled fashion in which his wife carried herself, perhaps partly due to the fact that she evidently cooked and cleaned and ironed and did all manner of housework until about 12:30am and then was up at 5:30am to prepare lunches for her husband and their four children. In their culture, she informed me, the husband had essentially zero responsibilities for the upkeep of the home or caring of the children. It seemed clear that her husband was getting many of his needs met from his relationship with his wife while in her relationship with him, a great deal was lacking for her.

Similarly, two members of a couple may produce very different Rope Trick responses.

While person A may produce a seemingly very happy or benign Rope Trick response, the other member of the couple, person B, may have a distinctly disturbing Rope Trick experience – or vice versa. The issue is not one of 'who is right and who is wrong', but rather it may be more accurate to invoke one of the most memorable lines of one of Bob Dylan's songs, *["One Too Many Mornings"]* when he sings, *"You're right from your side. I'm right from mine"*. In other words, both members of a couple may be 'right' from their own perspectives even if they clash with one another's. Indeed, that is one of the major advantages of carrying out the Rope Trick mental imagery exercise; by producing their own imagery sequences, the two persons may choose to share their experiences with one another and thereby illuminate for one another how each of them perceives their relationships at a particular point in time.

So far, representatives of *all* of the cultures I have had as clients indicated that they all share the same 'culturally patterned defect'.

Over the course of more than 40 years I have asked psychotherapy clients from many different cultures [including Greek, Israeli, Italian, Greek, French, German and numerous others] whether in their language and culture, when discussing the intimate relationship that he or she has with another person, whether they would refer to the two of them as having a single relationship or recognize that the relationship that person A has with person B may or may not be satisfactory to A, while the relationship that person B has with person A may also be satisfactory or not. I have yet to find a single individual from any culture or language who has indicated that in his or her culture and native language, that there is a recognition that at least two relationships are involved when speaking about the connections between two people. Should the reader be aware of any exception to this oft repeated error as far as his or her own language or culture is concerned, I would be pleased to learn of same; simply email me to wcupchik@aol.com .

A playwright's unique recognition of the fact that 'a relationship' actually resides <u>within</u> an individual

A remarkable recognition of the distinction between the relationship that one person has with the other from the relationship that the other has with the first person was inferred in the play written by Robert W. Anderson titled, *"I Never Sang For My Father"*. At the beginning of the play (and movie) the following statement is made: "Death ends a life, it does not end a relationship, which struggles on in the survivor's mind toward some resolution that it may never find." In other words, the relationship that person A has with person B is distinct from that which person B had with person A, and continues for A even after B is deceased.

Anderson's statement is, I believe, virtually unique in English literature; it also recognizes that the relationship that person A has with person B is not something 'out there' but rather resides *within* the individual, and is his or her own, and distinct from that which person B has with person A. Furthermore, even after one of them has died, the relationship that the surviving individual had with the deceased actually continues in a real sense, within the survivor's psyche and memory.

APPENDIX E

AN EXCEPTIONAL EXAMPLE OF THE SYMBOLIC MEANING OF A PHYSICAL OBJECT AND/OR ACTION

An important note: I happen to have another specialty in the field of psychology – namely, that having to do with the atypical theft behavior of usually honest persons [people who have often been wrongly diagnosed and labelled as suffering from kleptomania]. Over the past more than four decades I have often been interviewed by members of the print and electronic media who wanted to better understand why a celebrity or very financially well off individual would risk so much, in terms of personal reputation, professional standing, job, etc..., by shoplifting items worth relatively little, monetarily, compared to the perpetrators' readily available assets. During these interviews, including on ABC's **Good Morning America**, the CBS **Early Show**, and with the **New York Times**, **San Francisco Chronicle**, **PEOPLE** magazine, etc..., I have often illustrated the symbolic meaning of *why* a person stole *what* he or she stole, by providing real [yet camouflaged, of course] examples from my files of over 700 such cases.

The following case, while *not* an example involving the Rope Trick exercise, especially powerfully illustrates the symbolic meaning of an object [which the person happened to shoplift] more graphically than many other cases I have encountered over the years. Consequently, it can be instructive in assisting us all to appreciate that the unconscious may actually trigger behaviour which demonstrates, on an observable level, that actions and objects can have important symbolic meanings.

****

CASE # 11: VICTOR, AN HONEST MAN WHOSE SEEMINGLY NONSENSICAL ACT OF SHOPLIFTING CLEARLY DEMONSTRATED THE SYMBOLIC MEANING OF *WHAT* HE STOLE, *WHEN* AND *WHY*:

To illustrate the symbolic meaning of the atypical theft behaviour of usually honest persons, consider the case of Victor, a wealthy, retired business owner, who committed a totally unnecessary, single act of seemingly nonsensical and bizarre theft. His story has much to inform us about life, the lingering effects of early trauma and how the mind may deal symbolically with such, via his own remarkable acting out theft behaviour. I reported on this case in a previous book, yet it bears retelling now, for it offers what I believe is a truly classic, blatant example of the symbolic meaning that an everyday object may exemplify.

Victor was apprehended in the city of Los Angeles where he lived, in the spring of 1995, for shoplifting $15 worth of goods. What made the offence seem particularly bizarre was the fact that Victor was a very wealthy person who, as it became obvious upon investigation, also had no need whatsoever for the object that he stole.

As is true of many Holocaust survivors, Victor was an individual who had overcome incredible odds and horrific personal tragedy, and had strived and succeeded in becoming successful in his business and personal life, yet remained one for whom existence was permeated by a lingering aura of poignant pain, terror and sadness.

Everyone in Victor's family, including both his parents, his four younger siblings and all four grandparents, had been exterminated in the Nazi concentration camps during World War II. He recalled for me how, after they had tumbled out of the cattle car which had stopped just inside the gates of Auschwitz, his best friend had physically held him back from joining the line into which the Nazi soldiers had herded the rest of his family, and had told him to "stand up straight and look strong", so the German soldiers might think him potentially useful.

And indeed that is exactly what happened. Because he appeared to be a sturdy young boy, his life was saved so that he could do his captors' bidding. After the war was over and Victor was liberated, he was accepted for entry into the USA and began his life anew.

Victor had worked hard his entire adult life, eventually building his own successful business even as he married and became the father of three fine children, now all accomplished adults in their own right. Having been subjected to such depravity and injustice during his adolescent years in the camps, he afterwards consciously chose to honour his dear parents and other family members by living a highly ethical life. He was, therefore, more shocked than anyone when he offended against his own moral code of what was right and wrong, and was caught and charged for shoplifting on April 12, 1995. A few weeks later he was referred to me by a psychiatrist who was also a Holocaust survivor and who knew of my work on the forensic service of the Clarke Institute of Psychiatry with perpetrators of seemingly bizarre and nonsensical shoplifting behaviour.

When I interviewed Victor, at the time a senior citizen, he could not provide me with any reason or excuse whatsoever for his theft behaviour. He only recalled having entered a drugstore and then having placed an item in his coat pocket, at which point he proceeded to walk out of the store and was immediately apprehended.

Later on in our interview, as I was taking down his early history and he was describing his years in the concentration camps, he recalled for me his day of liberation. All the prisoners had been awakened in the middle of the night, and marched off into the dark outside of the camp's perimeter and along a rock-laden rail line vaguely lit by a crescent moon. They were sure that they were being marched to their deaths, probably to be shot in the woods and buried in a prepared pit, as had so many tens of thousands before them. He recalled that virtually none of the inmates were wearing shoes or any other foot-coverings as they had been so quickly rushed out of their barracks, and that his own feet were deeply bruised and bleeding as he staggered along. He recounted for me, almost matter-of-factly, that during the more than three hours of forced walking, those prisoners who fell down and were slow to get up, were immediately shot. Victor managed to stay on his feet and keep moving.

He said that after those horrifying hours of staggering along the rail line, the inmates were suddenly and without ceremony informed that the war was now over for them, that they were now free but that they should stay where they were as the Red Cross and Allied soldiers would soon arrive. Their Germans guards then ran away. Red Cross-marked trucks appeared near dawn and the prisoners' immediate needs were attended to, including the application of salves and bandages to their injured and bleeding feet.

The date of liberation, he mentioned in passing, was April 12, 1945. A few minutes later, I realized the import of what he had said and interrupted his continuing description of these events to ask, "When did you say you were liberated?"

"April 12, 1945," he said. And then, as he realized what he had said, an expression of shock followed by one of amazement flashed across his face. "Why, it's the same date that I stole!" he exclaimed, and he began to sob heart-wrenching tears. "Now," I inquired, "can you guess why it was that, 50 years to the day, on April 12, 19<u>95</u>, you entered a drug store and *stole a package of Dr Scholl's insoles* when you say that you had no need for the product, and could have easily paid for it - or for entirely new shoes for that matter - had you needed them?"

After another minute or more of now quiet sobbing, Victor softly replied, "For my feet, I suppose; my feet that were hurting so much... in 19<u>45</u>!"

Victor later said that ever since he arrived in the United States after the war, he always made certain that he had very adequate footwear; indeed, he always bought the best shoes he could afford, and prided himself on the fact that he always kept his shoes is excellent repair. He would *never* have required the item he stole, at least not in 1995!

Incidentally, Victor also expressed his certainty that he had not consciously recalled on the morning of his act of theft that it was the fiftieth anniversary of his day of liberation. He claimed to never allow himself to "waste time" thinking about his war experiences, and he never, *ever* discussed them with either his family or friends.

It is virtually certain, in my opinion, that Victor's unconscious had recognized that the date on which he stole was the 50th anniversary of his liberation and that he had experienced a severe 'anniversary reaction' that manifested in an act of [definitely atypical] theft behaviour, on April 12, 1995.

Some readers may recall that in 1995 there were very many commemorative events in the USA and elsewhere around the world related to the end of World War II generally, and in particular, of the Holocaust. Victor told me that he avoided being exposed to these proceedings as best he could; he did not want to have his memories and emotions aroused. But, while the memories of the horrors he experienced had been kept out of his conscious awareness, I believe it is virtually certain that his unconscious mind was fully aware of the significance of the date [April 12th] and was likely preoccupied with those memories at that time.

Had he actually needed insoles for a pair of his shoes he could certainly have afforded them. The fact is that he had no need for the item whatsoever. He did not steal the insoles for their *literal* value or intended use. However, the overwhelming *symbolic* value of acquiring the insoles is obvious; his unconscious clearly wanted the insoles to comfort his aching, bleeding feet of 50 years earlier.

****

OTHER BOOKS BY WILL CUPCHIK

Why Honest People Shoplift Or Commit Other Acts Of Theft
[Revised Ed., 2002]

Why Usually Honest People Steal [2013]

The Avro Arrow Manipulation: Murdering Medicare [A novel,
2005; Revised 2015]

REFERENCES

Cirlot, J. E. **A Dictionary Of Symbols**, Philosophical Library, Inc, 1962

Chekhov, Michael **To The Actor,** 1953

Cupchik, Will **Clinical Imaginative Imagery**, doctoral dissertation, University of Toronto, 1979

Cupchik, Will **Why Honest People Shoplift Or Commit Other Acts Of Theft**, 1997; Revised Edition, Tagami Communications, 2002

Cupchik, Will **Why Usually Honest People Steal**, Tagami Communications, 2013

Jung, Carl **The Collected Works of C.G. Jung, Vol. 18, The Symbolic Life**, 1975

www.ingramcontent.com/pod-product-compliance
Lightning Source LLC
Chambersburg PA
CBHW030023290326
41934CB00005B/463